"Using the voices of the survivors themselves, Dr. Finneran highlights the complexities of seeking and receiving help for domestic violence. The reader is provided with a macro level view of the professional services that are currently available as well as a blueprint for improving our system of care. The reader is also left with a better understanding of how to offer informal support to those we know and love who may be affected by interpersonal violence."

**Dr. Elena Welsh, Ph.D., Author of *Trauma Survivors' Strategies for Healing: A Workbook to Help You Grow, Rebuild, and Take Back Your Life***

"Dr. Michele Finneran's new book is a carefully crafted study of the role of formal and informal support for victims of domestic violence. One of the greatest tragedies in our families and communities is domestic violence. While domestic violence may start in the privacy of a home, it never remains there. Its impact bleeds out into the community, affecting neighborhoods, schools, and organizations. It requires the efforts of service providers, families, and friends to assist victims, yet too often lack of preparation and misinformation leave victims feeling misjudged, alone, and revictimized. Using the experiences and perspectives of domestic violence survivors regarding the services and support they received, Dr. Finneran provides important new information, recommendations, and approaches. Finally, we are hearing from survivors about what was helpful, what was not, and what they really needed. This is an important book filled with new hope and opportunities to make significant changes in how we serve and support those struggling with domestic violence. I highly recommend it!"

**Judith McKay, J.D., Ph.D., Associate Professor of Conflict Resolution & Community Studies, Nova Southeastern University**

# Surviving Domestic Abuse

*Surviving Domestic Abuse* examines how formal and informal supports and services can mitigate the damaging, and sometimes fatal, social cost of domestic violence. The book highlights victims' perceptions of supports and lays a foundation for professionals and family members to effectively assist victims of domestic abuse.

The book offers actionable recommendations and multiple-use cases to fill gaps in the understanding of the complexities that exist in domestic violence dynamics. Dr. Finneran uses real-life interviews with victims to inform action and intervention for policy, strategy and decision-making for support and service providers including law enforcement, healthcare, social services and employers. Identification of successful supports and services can assist in preventing victims from returning to their abusive relationships, and the author provides real-life examples and a sounding board for the voices of real women who have endured domestic abuse.

Spanning the gulf between research and practice, this is the ideal book for a range of professional communities including psychologists, social workers and healthcare professionals, and victims and survivors themselves. It's also suitable for academics and researchers, and students taking domestic violence treatment and prevention courses.

**Michele A. Finneran, Ph.D.**, is a Clinical Psychotherapist with Vecc & Associates, LLC. She has a Ph.D. in Conflict Resolution/Dispute Analysis from Nova Southeastern University. Dr. Finneran is licensed to practice in the state of Florida and her research and experience focuses on the topic of domestic abuse populations. She also emphasizes thought and mood disorders, as well as psychological and emotional issues in her clinical, private practice.

# Surviving Domestic Abuse

## Formal and Informal Supports and Services

**Michele A. Finneran, Ph.D.**

Routledge
Taylor & Francis Group
NEW YORK AND LONDON

First published 2021
by Routledge
52 Vanderbilt Avenue, New York, NY 10017

and by Routledge
2 Park Square, Milton Park, Abingdon, Oxon, OX14 4RN

*Routledge is an imprint of the Taylor & Francis Group, an informa business*



*Library of Congress Cataloging-in-Publication Data*
A catalog record for this title has been requested

ISBN: 978-0-367-85959-6 (hbk)
ISBN: 978-0-367-85958-9 (pbk)
ISBN: 978-1-003-01600-7 (ebk)

Typeset in Bembo
by Swales & Willis, Exeter, Devon, UK

This book is dedicated to my female family members, who survived domestic abuse in their own relationships and who inspired me to conduct research in this field and inspired me to write this book.

# Contents

# Acknowledgements

It is my hope that this book will become a pivotal part of a solution in the ongoing crisis of domestic abuse. Throughout my years of research in this field, I have learned that the system that is supposed to support victims of domestic abuse continues to be reactive, lacking and inadequate. Finally, the mission of this book is intended to be instrumental in victims' having a voice through sharing their stories and enlighten those who service/support victims of domestic abuse to become more proactive and empathetic.

I would like to acknowledge my gratitude and appreciation to the interviewed survivors of domestic abuse, who shared their stories and whose voices made this book possible. When victims shared their stories and tribulations, they gave others hope so they can overcome their own adversity. Thank you for your powerful voices. I would like to give a special thank you to Dr. Judith McKay for working with me and believing in me throughout the development of my academic coursework and research development. I would like to especially thank Dr. Lenore Walker for sharing her expertise, knowledge and insights in the field of domestic abuse. I would like to give a special thanks to Mrs. Natalie Vecchione, MS, MT-BC: Project Manager and Social Media Coordinator (aka "My Work Wifey") with Vecc & Associates; thank you for your encouragement, your ideas and brainstorming … and your love and support throughout this entire process. To my beloved husband, Brian C. Finneran; thank you for your unconditional love and ongoing support in seeing me through this vital project for me, you are loved beyond measure. To my phenomenal mom, Gilda A. Vecchione, I want to thank you for your lifelong love, encouragement and never-ending support, not only for this book, but throughout my entire life span. To my amazing dad, who taught me dreams can come true with hard work. I want to thank you for making opportunities happen for me from above. I would finally like to give a special thanks to my family members and friends who have promoted and listened to my ideas and praised my efforts in my attempt to make systemic changes in the field of domestic violence.

# Introduction

Domestic abuse is a leading source of relationship issues and a major driver of divorce and fatalities in the United States. In cases of domestic abuse, women (who are the most frequent victims) critically require appropriate, support services. Resources available to victims are formal supports and informal supports. Formal supports include: law enforcement, mental health professionals, medical staff, clergy and judiciary system. Informal supports can include: family, relatives, friends, coworkers and supervisors. Many victims have used both types of supports to stop the violence and leave their abusive partners, but not all support systems effectively work. Oftentimes, the efficacy of these providers of support and services are impaired by gaps in their understanding of the complexities and textures that exist in domestic abuse dynamics.

Abuse of women has no boundaries, no prejudices and abuse is evident by its ability to cross all social, racial, religious, ethnic and national lines. *Any woman can become a victim of domestic abuse.* Violence against women in intimate partner relationships remains one of the most critical issues that affects society. Researcher Mills (1998) defines domestic abuse as "an act by a partner resulting in physical harm, bodily injury, assault or physical and/or emotional threats that reasonably place the member in fear of such acts." Abusers will often utilize their power and control with overt threats, emotional abuse, using the children against the victim, financial control and utilizing male privilege … to name a few examples. Domestic abuse victims are often victimized more than once and findings suggest that domestic abuse is a serious criminal justice and public health concern. Domestic abuse has increasingly caused significant problems in our society within relationships involving interpersonal, physical and psychological problems for women in the United States and worldwide.

The rationale of this book is to identify how supports and services can be efficient in helping a victim leave her abuser. This book will also assist in helping providers and family with what is most effective in what they should and should not say to a victim, in order to be helpful and useful in escaping the realm of violence in the abusive relationship.

This book is divided into three parts. Part 1 describes the process of victims seeking help and the emotions attached to it. Seeking help is a difficult process for most who endure violent relationships as Zosky (2011) illustrates. The process of seeking outside help can be confusing for victims, due to the possibility of getting revictimized while seeking help. This part also explains the following:

- The ability for victims to become more vigilant and aware of the abuse.
- How domestic abuse is not portrayed as it is in the media (television, movies, etc.).
- Domestic abuse tends to evolve into a life-threatening situation.
- The feelings of humiliation that come over the victim, as a determinant of not seeking help.
- The emotional complexity of the domestic abuse dynamic by depicting Stockholm Syndrome and the victim's need to protect the abuser.

Part 2 of the book investigates formal supports and services that have been utilized in the midst of the victim alleviating her violent dynamic, and how helpful or unhelpful these formal supports and services were in accomplishing this goal. Finally, Part 3 focuses on informal supports, how productive were the family, relatives, friends, coworkers and employers with assisting the victim in abolishing the violent relationship.

The scope of this book focuses solely on heterosexual couples. However, further investigation and research can serve different sexual orientations within the realm of the same or similar topic. In addition, the scope of this book solely depicts the female as the victim and the male as the perpetrator. However, in today's era, more and more females are becoming the perpetrator/abuser, while more males are suffering in silence as the victim in a violent relationship.

The goal of this author is aimed directly at female victims who suffer domestic abuse in providing knowledge, different support options and ultimately … empowerment. In doing so, this author hopes to leverage victims' perceptions, reflections and feelings. Additionally, this book will document recommendations for policy, strategy and decision-making for supports and service providers. Identification of successful supports and services can assist in preventing victims from returning to their abusive relationships and will hopefully add to the current body of literature. There is a paucity of research on domestic abuse. Consequently, there is also a gap in the literature that exists regarding how victims perceive the help that they receive either formally or informally. Furthermore, there is a lack of knowledge of how and if these supports and services are effective. Many times, there are barriers for the victim in accessing resources, which leads her right back into the abuser's space.

This book provides actual examples and a sounding board for the voices of real women who have endured domestic abuse. They are represented underneath each title and subheading. It was imperative for this author to translate these semi-structured interviews, which were conducted with survivors of domestic abuse, in order to empower their voices. These interviews were conducted over a time frame of approximately six months. As a result, this author provides experiential information, view-points and knowledge from women who have endured domestic abuse. All domestic abuse survivors' names that were used in this book have been changed in order to secure confidentiality and protect their identities.

This book demonstrates victims' perceptions of utilized supports that can lay a foundation for professionals and family members to effectively help someone who is a victim of domestic abuse. This book can also be utilized as an educational guide and tool for professionals and service providers to determine how to ensure valuable services when serving domestic abuse victims and how to systematically treat this population. Based on empirical evidence, professionals need to be qualified, well-trained and educated to provide quality services to women who have survived domestic abuse. Inadequate professional preparation will only compound the level of ineffectiveness that leads to such intervention. As a result, many victims, who have endured negative experiences with formal supports and services, may feel uncomfortable in attempting to reach out and utilize formal supports and services again. This discomfort can lead to a fear of being revictimized by the professional (who may have well-intentions, but is in need of additional knowledge or training). Lastly, our society needs to be readily prepared when children, coming from homes of domestic abuse, become adults. Children that have been exposed to continuous domestic abuse have more of a tendency to repeat the same patterns as adults in their own families. Therefore, our society needs to be prepared for the repercussions of domestic abuse in families with supports and services that will provide preventive measures to stop the cycle of family violence and domestic abuse in households worldwide.

# Part 1

# Seeking Help

If there is one question that victims of domestic abuse often hear (from people who are either formal or informal supports), that question would be "Why don't you just leave the relationship?" This compounded question is the main premise and partial rationalization as to why women are initially resistant to seek help in the first place. This chapter will share victims' comments regarding the main reasons why they did not seek support earlier and the overall lack of awareness they encountered. By giving these victims voices to share their stories, they also shared their overall lack of awareness in not realizing their relationships were abusive. In addition, this chapter will summarize "Stockholm Syndrome," which emphasizes the victims' inability to psychologically break free from their abusers. Finally, victims comment on the complex, psychological process of Stockholm Syndrome.

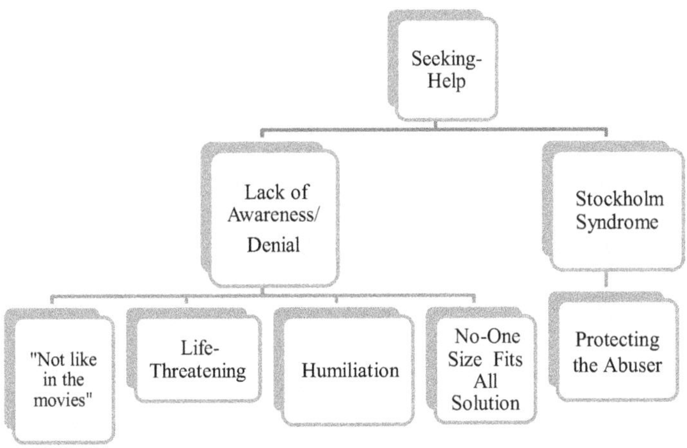


*Figure 1.1* Seeking Help

# 1 Seeking Help

## Lack of Awareness and Denial

The overall lack of awareness of victims of domestic abuse is significant, due to their inability in identifying the actual abuse and if they felt that their experiences were even considered abusive. Victims shared that violence escalated slowly and they did not recognize that what they were enduring was actual abuse. Some of the victims thought abuse was going to be a single episode or a different phase in the relationship that was triggered by stress. Some victims denied or did not perceive their relationships as being abusive. These victims may have felt something was wrong, but they could not pinpoint *what* exactly was wrong. Therefore, this ambivalence caused the victims to hesitate in making the conclusion that something truly was wrong. Some victims voiced that they did not even realize that anything was wrong and began to normalize the abuse. In some instances, victims did not identify what was happening was abuse and this *lack of awareness* that abuse was manifesting in their relationship prevented them from seeking help.

Melissa indicated that she was married for an eight-year period. She mentioned that she dated her husband for one year prior to being married. She said that she became engaged, married and had her first child all within a two-year period. She also commented that her abuse started out with verbal arguments, which eventually led to physical violence. Melissa shared that she never thought of getting any type of help for her abuse. She reported, "I did not think about getting some type of support in order to help myself or prevent the abuse from occurring." This reinforces the finding that many victims *do not realize that abuse is occurring*, as they don't identify their partners' behaviors as being abusive.

Monique met her partner when she was a teenager in high school. She indicated that she was married for 15 years and they had been together for 18 years. She reported that her abuse involved neglecting and ignoring, verbal abuse, being non-supportive of personal crises and incidences of physical abuse. Similarly, Monique indicated, "I did not know it was abuse that prevented me from seeking help; I didn't know anything was wrong." In Monique's case, she was not aware that what she was experiencing was considered abuse. As a result, this mindset prevented her from seeking help. At times, victims often disclose that they know "something" is wrong, but do not identify it as abuse, therefore, they never seek out help from supports.

When Cindy met her abuser, she was in her early twenties and her abuser was in his mid-thirties. She stated that she had been previously married with a child and they moved in together after a year. Cindy also mentioned that she did not have a job and had few business clients, whom were friends. Cindy was also unaware that she was being abused. She did not understand that what she was experiencing was abuse until she reported she "was in the midst of it." Cindy summarized, "I did not realize that I was being abused. I did not understand that kind of abuse, until you are in the middle of it, you don't know it at all." Cindy described when she was involved in her abusive relationship; she was unaware that it was abusive because of her involvement in the dynamic of the relationship. Cindy also admitted that she did not understand the true meaning of abuse, nor associated it with what she was experiencing. Many domestic abuse victims are in denial and do not want to believe they are being abused. They do not seek support until *others* bring it to their awareness. Cindy explained that she did not seek counseling because "I was in such denial with it before; it just did not even occur to me that I was in an abusive relationship."

Susan stated that she married her husband in order for him to stay in the country. She also did not label her experiences as domestic abuse. She felt as though it was more like sexual assault. Susan had some level of denial when talking about her relationship being physically violent. Susan stated, "I did not know to label it domestic violence. I still don't consider it domestic violence. It is more like sexual assault." Susan did not categorize her experiences as sexual assault encompassed in domestic abuse and failed to recognize these sexually abusive occurrences as part of the domestic abuse. She also let the sexual abuse override the physical abuse she endured; therefore, she did not consider it being domestic abuse. Many victims are unable to differentiate *what is* domestic abuse and *what is not* domestic abuse.

Denice was with her partner for nine years. She indicated that she was married to her ex-husband four years prior to leaving him. She relayed that it was her brother who called attention to the red flags in her partner: "my brother said that he (her husband) has symptoms of an abuser. Relying on what he would say to me, he validated what my other friends were saying, that I was in an abusive relationship." Denice listened to her brother, who told her that her husband was an abuser and explained the overall behaviors of an abuser. Other informal supports (who were around Denice) were seeing that her husband was abusive. Due to Denice's lack of awareness and her denial of her husband being abusive, she didn't listen to the concerns of other informal supports until her brother explained it to her. Many victims (like Denice) do not understand or recognize abuse for what it is, until it is explained in a way that the victims are able to receive that information.

Maria stated that her abuser was her boyfriend and they lived together and had a son together. She indicated that at the beginning of the relationship, she was getting divorced from a previous marriage. She stated that it was very fast, and she got pregnant within a couple of weeks of being with her abuser; "It was great for the first six months and all of a sudden he started getting more and more possessive and jealous." Maria explained that at first she did not realize anything being wrong until her abuser's ex-girlfriend showed up at their doorstep. Maria listened to what the ex-girlfriend had to say:

> I did not realize that anything was wrong at first, until his ex-girlfriend showed up and said "I have flashbacks, panic attacks and I cannot sleep at night, I want my dignity and self-respect back. I want everything that he took from me." His ex-girlfriend told me that he hit her all the time, even while she was pregnant. She was saying she had a miscarriage because of him. That is when things changed for me, when his ex-girlfriend showed up.

Maria again was not aware, until she witnessed her abuser's ex-girlfriend in such distress, that the abuser was doing the same thing to her as he did to his ex-girlfriend. As a result from this incident, she developed a sense of reality and acute awareness of what she experienced.

As previously noted from the victims' accounts, many of them were completely unaware that something was wrong. If they did understand something was wrong, they did not consider it abuse. It was not until something or someone significant showed them that they were being abused. This *lack of awareness* prevented victims from realizing the abuse or even defining it as such, which hindered them from seeking help in the first place.

## Not like in the Movies

Women who have endured domestic abuse perceived the abuse as how it is portrayed in the media. Television, books and movies often portray domestic abuse as constant aggressiveness, bloodshed and brutalization. However, many victims, based on their experiences, believe that domestic abuse is wrongly portrayed in the media versus domestic abuse "real life" scenarios. For example, Maria described her idea of what she felt domestic abuse was: "I felt that if I was not being strangled or beaten to death, it felt like this was a minor case. I felt that my case did not warrant support. I was not murdered or attempted to be murdered." Maria had a stereotypical perception of domestic abuse, based on media portrayal of domestic abuse. She felt that if she was not on the brink of death, her situation did not warrant attention.

In movies, such as *The Burning Bed* and *Sleeping with the Enemy*, domestic abuse is the primary focus. Nonetheless, it is depicted that the victim had to reach extreme deadly measures for it to be defined as domestic abuse. However, the reality of domestic abuse is *any* type of emotional, physical and/or sexual abuse that may or may not result in brutalization, constant physical or emotional tormenting for it to be considered abusive. Maria explained,

> I did not know anything about domestic violence. You see in the movies these girls getting punched, I was not getting punched. I was getting slapped and pushed around. I did not know that is what it was. I was seeing it on TV and felt like since he was not breaking my jaw, then I am not in a domestic violence situation. I really did not know.

Maria described her abuse as "*little facial slaps of humiliation*," or "*two hour screaming matches*," where her abuser criticized everything that she did from driving to shopping.

This unrealistic media portrayal prevents women, who have endured abuse, to seek help initially. *Domestic abuse is viewed, in our societal culture, as being a spontaneous act or acts. A more realistic view of domestic abuse is that it often occurs slowly – beginning with emotional and/or mental abuse, which can lead to escalation and increase tension building between partners manifesting into more severe, physical abuse. This is all done with an element of manipulation, power and control tactics utilized by the abuser.*

## Life-Threatening

Many women who endure abuse do not seek help to get out of their relationships until the relationship becomes life-threatening to them or their families. For many victims to escape, the relationship has become too volatile (mentally, emotionally, physically and/or sexually) for the victims to think about discontinuing their relationship. Many women, who endured abuse, continued with their toxic relationships until things took a turn of disparity and "ending of life" scenarios.

Cindy described:

> I feared that I was not going to wake up. He was a pill user and knocked himself out. I was safe, but I did not feel safe at the time. It got to the point that you think you are going to die.

Cindy was scared for her life, since her abuser was so erratic and unpredictable, especially when he was under the influence of drugs. However, she realized that because of her abuser's addiction, she had more of a chance of not dying because of his blacking out from abusing pills. Many times, the victim is known to make several attempts to leave the relationship only to come back to the abuser. They even could visualize their own deaths, as a result of the development of their abuse becoming more of a threat to their lives. Melissa indicated that "at the end of the day and climax [...] he basically tried to kill me and leave me to die."

Stacy also feared for her own life and the lives of her loved ones. She felt a threat for their safety and said "If I had gone to the court two and a half months prior, we would not be in this position. I felt like I would have been dead, along with my family right now." Stacy felt that both she and her family members were endangered by the severity and complexity of the abuse. *This is a blockade which again prevents victims from seeking help.*

Laura discussed that she was forced into her relationship and marriage, as her abuser was continuously threatening her and her child. Laura realized that she was in a domestic abusive relationship when she was faced with death. For Laura, it did occur to her to reach out previously; she reported however, that she was in such denial looking back on her abusive relationship, "I did not realize that I was in a domestic violence relationship until it got so severe that I had to go to a shelter, but I did not understand the relationship being potentially fatal." For Laura, Stacy and Cindy, the realization was *not until the abuse became so severe that their lives were at risk and death was impending* if they did not seek out help. When their circumstances became brutal and violent, they finally reached out for help ... but only at that time. These victims were facing death and they became instinctively aware that they needed to dissolve their relationships in order to save themselves and/or their families.

## Humiliation

Many victims felt embarrassed or humiliated in speaking with others about their abuse. Victims can be embarrassed, as they think that formal and informal supports would "look down on them". The overall notion of having someone being abusive toward them is humiliating for victims. Maria shared, "If I did not feel so humiliated, I would have told more people. It is that you are looked down as a victim; that is something that happens to trashy people, right?" Maria felt as though she could not have told more people, since she was concerned about what other people thought of her. She indicated that she would have earlier reached out to supports for help, but she felt ashamed and humiliated in doing so.

Cindy distracted herself from her relationship being intentionally involved in other things because she felt ashamed and humiliated being a part of an abusive relationship. Some victims do not want to inform their family members, since their family members would be disapproving. Cindy stated, "My family did not know that we were living together ... they thought I was living with friends. I lived a double life." Some family members did not know their daughters' involvement or details of their destructive relationships, until their daughters made them aware.

Victims did not reach out for supports or did not speak out due to their humiliation and embarrassment that they experienced being involved in an abusive dynamic. Therefore, it can be noted that interviewed victims felt the social stigma of domestic abuse and their perceived outlook of what a "victim" looks like prevented them from seeking help (either earlier in their abusive relationships or at all). Anita indicated that her abusive relationship started in high school and lasted for ten years. She reported that she ended up marrying her partner, even as the verbal violence continued. Anita recalled from early in the relationship, there was a lot of screaming and arguing back and forth. She stated that after the birth of her son, the relationship began to get more emotionally abusive and became physically abusive. Anita expressed, "I was embarrassed to seek help and to speak out."

Natasha was in her twenties and coming out of another relationship that had all the potential to become abusive. At first, she shared that she and her partner did not have a "relationship title". She stated that she could not deal with anything and never considered herself as "fragile." Natasha indicated that when the abuse began, she

> did not tell anybody. I did not have too many people to count on and I did not want people to know. It was a very shameful situation to tell people that someone is beating on you. It is not something that you want to talk about.

Many victims feel the same way as Natasha and they do not want to voice their abuse to supports because of the humiliation and embarrassment attached to being a victim, another reason that prevents victims from seeking help. They feel ashamed, humiliated and embarrassed about their partners abusing them and that they were experiencing victimization.

## No "One-Size-Fits-All" Solution

Many women who suffer from victimization had experienced it differently. How the victimization was experienced correlated with how the abuse unfolded, the types of supports the victims had received and the process of seeking out help. Victims perceived their formal or informal supports as either effective or ineffective in assisting them to end their abusive relationships. However, there is no "one-size-fits-all" solution in effectively assisting victims. Individuals, who are part of formal and informal supports, need to understand that what might work well for one victim may not be effective for another victim. Additionally, those involved in both formal and informal supports need to view assisting a victim as an *intrinsically, individualized experience with specific treatment and support tailored to that unique victim.*

Jennifer shared, "I felt my situation was different … supports needed to understand my case was individualized. The things that might make sense to everyone might not make sense for the victim going through it, like to be rational." Many supports fail in understanding "how" and "why" victims cannot leave their abusive partners, even when the abuser is inflicting emotional and physical pain on them. Jennifer understood that each domestic violence case is different and that the feelings and thoughts of one victim may not apply to another victim.

Maria reported that, "people can tell you things that seem obvious. It is hard to hear it and then to do it." Maria also felt that people can tell the victim obvious and rational things to do, however, having the victim hear and implement these suggestions is difficult for the victim for a multitude of reasons. Formal and informal supports need to set an individualized, strategic plan for the victim, in order to recover from victimization by the abuser. A strategic plan is essential for the victim's well-being and safety. Having a "one-size-fits-all" mentality prevents victims from seeking help, since victims feel like they are receiving the same, standardized help of all victims of domestic abuse. It is paramount that the services, formal and informal supports should clearly be *individualized* and based on each victim's unique needs.

So far, Chapter 1 has addressed the following:

- The lack of awareness and denial that victims experience and not knowing what is even considered abuse.
- The lack of realization that the victim perceives as the experience is abusive in nature also results as a barrier in seeking initial help.
- Victims of domestic abuse also had a "false sense of reality" in that their situations were not considered abuse, since their experiences were not similar as portrayed in the media.
- The feelings of humiliation and social stigma experienced by the victims who endured such violence, as primary reasons why victims are so hesitant to receive help.
- Victims also felt the inability to seek help, since they felt like they were treated like "just another victim."
- The victims' view of the formal and informal support systems having this "one-size-fits-all" methodology was contraindicative to each of the individual victim's needs.

The above examples are some of the main reasons why victims of domestic abuse find it so difficult to reach out and seek help to end their abusive relationships.

## Stockholm Syndrome

During August of 1973 in Stockholm, Sweden, two bank robbers held three women and one man hostage for 131 hours. After their rescue, it became apparent that the hostages were not responding in a way that was expected of typical hostages (Lambert, 2019). The hostages showed support for their captors and shielded them from the police. Afterwards, the hostages refused to testify against them, raised money for their defense and even visited them in prison. This event and resulting condition became known as "Stockholm Syndrome". This condition is recognized as a coping mechanism used by individuals in hostage situations. It can also be used to understand the "bonding" that takes place in other abusive situations, for example, prisoners of war, children who have been physically or sexually abused, cult members and victims of domestic abuse (Lambert, 2019). Research indicates that the longer amount of time that the hostages stayed with the captor, the more likely this "bonding" will begin. This is the same type of bonding found in a domestic abusive dynamic as outsiders are dumbfounded as to why they stay attached. This section will explain and answer why victims may stay in an abusive relationship.

This emotional bonding that takes place between hostage and captor is comparable to women living with an abusive partner. Kirkwood (1993) explained that it is traditionally a mental way of dissociating with the feelings of anxiety, fear and helplessness by seeing the situation almost through the lens of the abuser. It is considered a subconscious survival strategy. Dutton and Painter (1993) used the term "traumatic bonding" to describe this strong emotional attachment. They describe that a victim living with domestic abuse is intermittently assaulted and/or threatened by the abuser, who then will be alternatively warm, kind and loving. Since no alternative relationship is available to the victim, the victim tends to bond and focus more on the positive side of the abuser. Kirkwood (1993) indicated that Stockholm Syndrome does not occur in every hostage situation, however he specified four conditions that need to be identified in order for Stockholm Syndrome to take place:

- Perceived extreme threat to physical or psychological survival.
- Perceived inability to escape.
- Isolation from other perspectives than that of the captor.
- Perceived small kindness from the captor (letting the hostage live is enough).

Stockholm Syndrome is considered a psychological phenomenon, where hostages can relate and identify with their captors. Graham et al. (1995) suggested that the Stockholm Syndrome experienced by hostages provided a useful model for understanding the experience and behavior of women living with domestic abuse. Kirkwood (1993) also implied that Stockholm Syndrome demonstrated how the power imbalance between abusers and victims can result in this strong, intense emotional bonding. He also concluded that research has shown that the effects on women who experience this syndrome as having: low self-esteem, dependence upon the abuser, feelings of hopelessness about ending the violence, a tendency to minimize or deny the violence and a wedge or space between victims and the supports who are attempting to help or rescue them.

The parallels between Stockholm Syndrome and domestic abuse can be models for formal and informal supports who need to learn and understand why this psychological hold can prevent a victim of domestic abuse from leaving the abuser. Learning about this condition can assist individuals, who are either formal or informal supports, in the process of working more *efficiently* and *proactively* with women who suffer from domestic abuse. As in the Stockholm Syndrome, the victim of domestic abuse perceives the abuser as controlling and manipulating in her life and can have the potential to become a deadly situation. The abuser makes the victim aware of this by his words and actions either directly or indirectly. Wallace (2007) stated the abuser can be physically abusive to the victim or other family members, or can damage property in front of the victim, leaving a sense of fear for the victim. The abuser uses direct or indirect threats and emotionally damaging comments, which also endanger the victim's survival. The victim feels that she is unable to escape this psychological trap. Individuals who do not understand this condition cannot comprehend why a victim of domestic abuse is still involved in the abusive dynamic. One of the main reasons why a victim stays is not only because of the "emotional attachment and bonding," but also the financial component and emotional time invested in the abuser. Often, the victim feels the inability to live independently, since she does not have direct access to funds or does not know her financial status and as a result has no way of living without the abuser. Furthermore, a victim of domestic abuse may perceive she has invested a lot of time and mental energy in attempting to fix the abuser and the thought of starting over in a new relationship is a daunting notion. The victim may even experience overt threats from the abuser, hearing phrases like, "I will kill you, or take my own life and it will be your fault." As a result of these threats, the victim loses her self-esteem and self-confidence that comes with feeling trapped and having no way out. Consequently, victims of domestic abuse can easily develop comorbid mental illnesses, such as depression, anxiety, PTSD and other relevant mental health symptoms that are caused by the terrorism of their abusers.

Within the Stockholm Syndrome, captors (victims) tend to be locked away from other people and society and any outside influences. The victim is monitored by the abuser, leaving her to feel extremely isolated and alienated from family, friends or associates. Kirkwood (1993) indicated that the captive (victim) is expecting violence or to be killed, so any instances of reduction or violence, such as friendliness, or letting the hostage (victim) live after threatening to kill her, are taken as signs that the captor (or abuser) is "not all bad" (Lambert, 2019). Graham et al. (1995) reported that

> with the perception of kindness and hope, the victim denies any feelings of danger, terror or rage that the abuser creates in her and such denial allows the victim to commence in bonding to the positive side of the abuser.

As a result, the victim views that the abuser is not "all that bad" and the victim develops hope and a willingness to work on improving the relationship. The victim might want to experience the "honeymoon phase." This is a phase, after the enduring abuse by the abuser, that consists of apologies, gift giving, compliments, being kind at that moment, giving the victim permission to be with her children and family and not abusing her when she expects it. Individuals (outside of the relationship) may view this as a healthy and a typical relationship, however, they are unaware of unhealthy factors and abusive dynamics. The victim is also searching for times when the abuser is "not all that bad." Kirkwood (1993) identifies four conditions that can result in beliefs and behaviors by the victim:

- An overwhelming need to pacify the abuser in order to survive.
- The victim adopts the abuser's perspective and his lens.
- Intense feelings of gratitude toward the abuser.
- The victim rejecting support, help, or rescue which the victim perceives would aggravate the abuser.

Acknowledgement of these common beliefs and behaviors can increase formal and informal supports' willingness and understanding why victims feel like they cannot leave or do not desire to leave. Ultimately, this knowledge will increase the ability in how to help the victim. Stockholm Syndrome is described in a domestic abuse context as an unhealthy bond between the victim and the abuser. In terms of how the traumatic bonding between abuser and victim occurs, it essentially needs to be broken emotionally from the abusive ties for the victim's livelihood and continued existence. It is a vicious cycle – the victim develops the unhealthy bond to *survive* in the abusive relationship, yet it prevents her from taking the necessary steps to *end* the abusive relationship. Many victims that experience Stockholm Syndrome progress through four stages of victimization by: minimizing the abuse, suppression of their own anger, dependent behavior on the abuser and rage and fear when separated from the abuser, which Walker (2016) coined as the "Battered Woman Syndrome." For many victims, there is forced isolation and alienation from their informal supports by the abuser. Alternately, some victims do not experience forced isolation or alienation. However, the interpersonal skills, confidence and social relationships of the victims of domestic abuse are negatively impacted, thus making it hard for the victims to connect with people. The victims internally feel isolated and alienated as they carry around this secret because of how they believe others will perceive them. As a result, relationships with long-term friends or family are broken and victims tend to isolate themselves not only because of how they are being perceived, but also from the strict monitoring and overseeing of the abuser. This makes it extremely difficult for victims to seek help from formal and/or informal supports.

Many victims do experience Stockholm Syndrome as the abuser's protector, as well as someone who would guard the abuser if he had to face consequences. Some victims also have tendencies to show care, concern and sympathy for their abusers. This makes it very confusing for those involved as formal or informal supports to comprehend how or why victims are feeling this way … especially since the abuser is inflicting emotional, physical and sexual pain onto the victim.

Police calls of domestic violence scenes are probably the most dangerous because law enforcement officers are dealing with the abuser (the one inflicting pain on the victim), and the victim (the one protecting the abuser from the police). Often, there are cases where the victim then attacks the police officer, who is attempting to protect them from the abuser.

Maria describes the psychological complexity of the dynamic:

> It is the Stockholm Syndrome. The police don't understand it at all … They don't know how to deal with domestic violence because they don't understand the way we think. You don't know that you are being abused because they have us so brainwashed; the only voice in your head is your abuser. It is like you are an idiot; you get withdrawals when you leave them. You are addicted to being abused. You are addicted to being controlled. Someone is telling me what to do. I don't have to think, people don't understand, it is so crazy.

## Protecting the Abuser

Many victims, who suffer from Stockholm Syndrome, have sort of an identification with the abuser, as well as feeling the need to be protective of him. Katie was married to her abuser for four years and together with him for eight years. The abuse, during the marriage, consisted of her abuser controlling what she did and being very manipulative. Katie described the physical abuse occurring approximately five times as incidences consisting of him being aggressive with her, both physically and verbally, as well as physically trying to remove her from combative situations. She shared how she called the police when the last incident became physically abusive:

> The last incident when he threw me into the car, it was no question; the police showed up and asked me: "What happened?" I said, "My

> husband just picked me up and threw me into the car." The police continued to question the marks on my arms as I had marks all over. I was completely shaken up and a complete wreck. They were like, "that's it, we are taking him." I was like, "no, no you cannot take him." Even when they were taking him away in the cop car, I was feeling like my heart was being ripped out of my chest, like what did I do? Why did I do this? I really believed all the things he had told me … I should not have called the police. I should have let it go again and again.

From Katie's statement, it was apparent that she was feeling the need to protect her abuser from law enforcement. She was able to identify with her abuser in feeling sympathy for him for getting him in trouble with the law. She also indicated that she felt guilty and remorseful for making the police call in the first place.

Karen stated that her abuser was her high school sweetheart. She lived in his neighborhood and married him in her early twenties. She reported that she was with him for 20 years (and separated for two years). Karen had a no-contact order against her abuser. She was not legally permitted to have any type of contact with her abuser, but she had contacted him anyway and went against the order. Karen shared that she felt incredibly fearful, anxiety-ridden and panicked all the time: "I was allowing him to have the kids once every other weekend and after that he would contact me and come over the house." Many times, the abuser had faced consequences by the victim, such as incarceration or him spending money to hire a lawyer to go through the court system. Victims expressed that they felt this way because they did not want to experience more emotional, financial or physical repercussions from the abuser. Similarly, Anita expressed:

> I was afraid that if I did not get the restraining order things would have been worse for me at home, because it has escalated to the point that I told the judge that he rules the relationship with fear and intimidation.

Jennifer stated that through it all, she continued to have compassion and empathy towards her abuser, as well as to "trying to cure him". She compared her abuser to a sick cancer patient who needed help. This perception is also true of Stockholm Syndrome.

Jennifer added:

> I felt sorry for him. I almost felt as if I was with someone who is sick, like cancer. I would not leave them. It sounds crazy. It was my thought process. He did need me. I spent so much time and did a lot to save him and fix his mistakes.

Jennifer is another example of a victim who experienced Stockholm Syndrome and the need to protect her abuser. She was able to identify her abuser's violent *episodes* and compare him to someone who was sick with a *medical condition*. She indicated that she spent time and energy attempting to save him, fix him and take care of him when he needed her. This is a psychologically, distorted combination: lack of awareness, denial, humiliation and "abuse until it becomes life-threatening". The factors of the "one-size-fits-all" solution in dealing with victims, Stockholm Syndrome and the victims' need protect their abusers *all* made it a struggle and challenging for victims of domestic abuse to seek support.

Part 2 depicts formal supports that were used when victims did reach out and seek help. These formal supports consist of law enforcement, mental health/social services, medical staff, clergy and judicial system and how effective/ineffective these supports were in assisting the victims in eradicating their abusive relationships.

# Part 2

# Formal Supports

Formal supports are defined as professional supports that are geared to work and assist victims of domestic abuse. As shown in Figure 2.1, formal supports in this chapter consists of: law enforcement; mental health/social services; medical staff/clergy and judicial system (which also includes attorneys being part of the judicial/legal system).

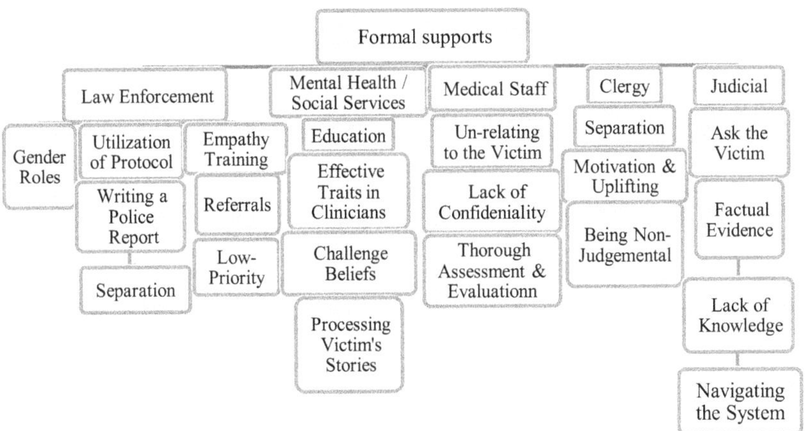


*Figure 2.1* Formal Supports

# 2 Law Enforcement

Law enforcement is typically described as an organized system in society that enforces the law by punishing or rehabilitating those individuals who violate the laws of society. Examples included in law enforcement: police officers, local municipalities, detectives and hostage negotiators. Within this chapter, the following sub-categories are described:

- Gender Role: which depicts how the gender of the police officer affects the victims in a domestic violence situation.
- Utilization of Protocol: The importance of the use of protocol performed by law enforcement and its impact on victims.
- Police Report: The application of having law enforcement make a police report.
- Separation: Law enforcement separating the victim from the abuser at the scene.
- Empathy Training: The need for empathy and sensitivity training provided for law enforcement, when assisting victims of domestic abuse.
- Low Priority: The concept that some victims perceive how law enforcement officers feel about these types of domestic abuse calls.

## Gender Roles

The gender of the law enforcement officers (that are responding to domestic abuse situations) is significant to the victims of domestic abuse. The victims of domestic abuse expressed their increased comfort level when discussing the incidents with a female officer versus a male officer. Some victims perceive female officers as being more empathetic and supportive listeners.

Jennifer shared:

> I contacted the police; she was a female officer and she stated, "You don't understand what you are going through, you cannot see it, but you need to get out. This is not healthy." The female officer insisted

> that I get looked over by the paramedics … She was the only officer that showed compassion; the others did not.

Jennifer and other victims experienced female officers who tried to counsel and advise victims of what they needed to do for themselves, in order to break away from the cycle of domestic abuse. Based on Jennifer's experience, she shared that she found the female officer (who responded to her call) extremely helpful and compassionate toward her and her situation. Jennifer felt it was vital that the officer took the time to talk to her about what she needed to do and what she was experiencing as a victim in an domestic abusive relationship. Jennifer also thought it was helpful that the female officer medically cleared her, which showed Jennifer that the officer cared and she had concern for her medical condition.

Jennifer also stated:

> She (female detective) was good when she came out. I went out to my car, and this female detective came out and got me. She said, "Just come in and we will talk." She and I spoke a little bit. She was more helpful than they (male officers) and was more understanding. She followed me home and asked me if she felt comfortable taking her police car or not. She wanted to follow me and she wanted to come in and I would not let her. She said that she wanted to make sure no one else was there. She was really helpful and she was really nice.

Jennifer and other victims expressed they had "poor experiences" with male (law enforcement) officers, who did not seem overly helpful in relation to their victimization and situations. Jennifer (and other victims) re-emphasized that the female detective/female officers were extremely helpful and protective of her, as evidenced by following her home and requesting her to come into the house to make sure no one else was present. Jennifer explained that the detective also assessed her comfort level by following her in a civilian car instead of a marked car. Jennifer reported that she found it comforting that the female police officer wanted her to feel safe when she got home. Jennifer and other victims noted that gender (of the law enforcement officers) made a difference in the way victims were being responded to, listened to and treated by this type of formal support. Oftentimes, victims shared that they perceived male law enforcement officers as being "uncomfortable" in assisting victims of domestic abuse. Consequently, victims of domestic abuse interpret male officers, who may seem uncomfortable, as "not caring as much" for their emotional states and abusive situations.

Stacy thought the male officer (who responded to her call) was uncomfortable in talking with her about her domestic abusive situation. Stacy, in sensing the discomfort of the responding male officer, felt she would have been better off communicating with a female officer. She reported, "I felt that he (male police officer) was uncomfortable because of the situation or maybe that I would feel more comfortable talking to a woman about this situation." Stacy observed the male police officer's level of discomfort, particularly as she was speaking to him and recognized that she would have been better off speaking to a female officer about her abusive experience.

However, Cindy shared that she *did* have a female officer and Cindy wanted the female officer to sit with, console and comfort her … but she was disappointed when the female officer did not do that. Cindy stated, "The female officer did not console me at all. I thought the female officer was going to sit with me, and the male officer would investigate." Cindy desired for the female officer to show compassion and spend some time with her, while the male officers were assessing and investigating the situation with the abuser.

The victims of domestic abuse have *different expectations of* female law enforcement officers than they do of male ones. It is important for female police to assist and to reassure and relate and show solicited support toward victims. The gender role of law enforcement is important, as many victims thought female officers would proceed with being emotionally sensitive, advising and supporting the victim at the scene.

Based on the previous statements of the victims, overall recommendations for female law enforcement officers would be:

- Spending time with the victim at the scene.
- Assisting the victim and attempting to understand her individual needs.
- Giving words of encouragement.
- Providing support.
- Empathizing with what the victim is experiencing both physically and emotionally.

When female police officers provide these supportive measures for a victim of domestic abuse, it gives the victim a sense of empowerment and an opportunity for validation from the female police officer. Victims expressed that these measures of support are highly needed, in order to attain a level of encouragement and empowerment from this formal support.

Most of the interviewed victims felt that the female police officers were more empathetic or supportive … and overall more helpful towards victims of domestic abuse. The victims' perception was that a female officer should have more understanding and compassion towards them (based on gender role). When the female officers did not demonstrate this understanding and compassion, it left victims of domestic abuse feeling unsupportive and alone. *Another recommendation would be law enforcement dispatching both female and male officers to a domestic abuse call.* Again, this is based on the victims' experiences of how they perceived female officers who may be able to relate better to the victim (based on gender).

## Utilization of Protocol and Procedures

Many of the victims thought that law enforcement officers who followed certain protocols and procedures were better trained and more organized in handling such a volatile situation. When law enforcement officers instructed and explained to the victim the necessary next steps that they needed to do in order to protect themselves, victims found this guided instruction extremely helpful. Examples of this would be explaining how to obtain a restraining order from the courts, changing their name on the lease, etc. Many victims felt reassured and comforted when law enforcement followed a certain protocol in assisting them. When police officers were nonchalant about the given situation and did not provide instructions for the victim, the victims felt unsupported.

Stacy, Susan and Carol collectively agreed and shared similar sentiments: "I contacted the police who told me to take pictures of his stuff. The police were called and they explained that he needed to pay child support or he will be put in jail," or "I went to the police and asked them what to do in this case, and they said it was stalking. They advised me to go to the courts because it can get very serious… very quickly."

These are examples of how law enforcement officers guided the victims and instructed them to protect themselves … and these officers were deemed extremely helpful. When law enforcement responds to a call, the victim of domestic abuse is in a panicked state of mind and she may not be able to think clearly for herself. However, when law enforcement officers give a victim step-by-step instructions and guidance, it makes the necessary steps (for the victim's safety) *clear* and *tangible.*

It is also helpful when law enforcement assesses how many times the abuse has taken place for the victim, since often the abuse is not just a singular occurrence. Law enforcement officers need to understand (from the victims) the frequency and some of the dynamic of the victim and abuser's relationship. Katie indicated, "They went inside to talk to him. The police officers asked questions to me like, 'Was I hit? Did this happen before?'" Gathering this information, from the victim, is important for law enforcement officers to know the frequency, severity and level of violence that is occurring in the home currently and that has previously occurred.

The following section highlights protocols and procedures, such as the importance of writing a detailed and accurate police report and the act of separating the victim and abuser while doing their investigation. These protocols are imperative for the victim and to better assist in building the victim's case for court.

## Writing a Police Report

Law enforcement officers are inundated with the insurmountable paperwork that they need to complete for their job and during a police call. From a law enforcement perspective, paperwork can seem daunting and discouraging. Unfortunately, law enforcement officers' time and focus are less on the crime or warranted arrest and more on the amount of paper that is required of them by upper administration. However, writing a police report and having supportive documentation of a crime on the scene is necessary in all cases, especially with domestic abuse cases. When attending a domestic abuse call, the need for law enforcement to construct an accurate and thorough police report of the victimization is crucial. An accurate and detailed report from a domestic abuse call is deemed necessary and important for the victim's case. However, there may be times when this process and documentation does not occur or if it does the report is not accurate or detailed.

The primary reason why a police report needs to be obtained and accurate is for the victim to present within the court system. Victims need to have accurate, legal documentation to present to the judge in the legal system. In addition, it is important for an accurate and detailed record of the violence that occurred in the home (at that address) between the victim and abuser. Another reason why a police report is vital is that it can open up more avenues of funding for victims in a social service setting. For example, the written documentation by law enforcement can provide additional, more affordable treatment options for victims, as well as extensive access to formal supports and services.

Many victims were disappointed and discouraged when law enforcement arrived at the call, but failed to do an investigative interview and take the statements of the victim and abuser and did not complete a police report regarding the crime. Anita summed up, "The police were not writing anything down and never said that someone would contact me. It seemed like they did not care." It is helpful for victims for law enforcement officers to conduct separate interviews and write up an accurate police report, not only for the above reasons, but also to show intent of protection and follow-through on the given domestic abuse situation. Cindy felt frustrated when she asked for the police report and they told her that they were unable to provide her with one. She stated, "When I asked for a police report, he (the police officer) told me he could not give me a police report." This left Cindy feeling confused and bewildered, as well as unsupported. In Cindy's situation, the police officer did not provide a reason to Cindy as to why he would not write the report. Instead, he told her that he was unable to provide a report and he gave no explanation why. Many victims experience frustration towards law enforcement officers when they do not provide written documentation. Additional frustration is also experienced, by victims of domestic abuse, when law enforcement officers neglect to provide, in the report, actual evidence of how the crime was committed or how domestic abuse occurred at the scene.

Karen expressed disappointment when law enforcement wrote a report, yet neglected to include domestic abuse as the cause of conflict and crime in the home. As previously stated, incomplete or inaccurate police reports can prevent victims from getting victims' compensation or funding. Karen said, "When they wrote the police reports, they wrote only for the sexual abuse crimes. This did not allow me to get victims' compensation, a $1500 relocation compensation for any victim of domestic violence." Making sure that the police report has accurate information and that the victim reads over the police report prior to law enforcement leaving is highly recommended.

According to another victim, since there was sexual violence of her child by the abuser, the victims' domestic abuse case was overlooked due to the sexual abuse of a minor. Sexual abuse of a minor superseded and overrode the severity of the domestic violence for the victim. Laura indicated,

> My daughter told the officers about the sexual abuse she endured. The whole domestic abuse unit leaves, and the whole sexual assault crimes unit comes in … and to this day, they did not prosecute him (the abuser) for domestic violence, only sexual abuse.

In this case, both domestic abuse and sexual assault units needed to have involvement: the domestic abuse unit interviewing the victim (mother), and sexual assault unit interviewing the daughter (minor). Both the sexual assault *and* domestic abuse need to be documented, in order to create a stronger case (against the abuser) in the court system.

In summary, having law enforcement write a police report that is accurate and detailed, after interviewing both the victim and abuser is highly recommended for the previously stated reasons.

## Separation

Victims experienced the benefits of effective protocol and practices when law enforcement were able to *separate* the victim from the abuser (and prevent them from interacting) during the investigative interview. Nancy stated that she met her abuser and married him only a month later; she said that their relationship progressed very quickly. She later realized that he married her for his citizenship. Nancy expressed that she had to call 911 for assistance because of their abusive relationship. Nancy shared, "I called 911 and they separated us. One officer spoke to me; as the other officer spoke to my husband. I tried to give them a quick summary of what was going on in my life with this man." Nancy felt that the separation was necessary and helpful in order for her to be able to speak freely about what was occurring with her abuser. In instances when law enforcement did not physically separate the victim from the abuser, victims expressed a level of discomfort in not being able to talk freely and openly with law enforcement (while the abuser was in the room or even within earshot of the victim). Stacy explained, "The police did not separate us. The police took our statements like it was nothing. They did not separate us … I felt like we should not have been in the same room." It is highly recommended that law enforcement, when getting statements from both parties, physically separate the victim from the abuser. This separation is essential, in order for the victim not to feel intimidated or fearful of having the abuser hear the victim's statements. While separated, the victim and abuser cannot be within earshot of each other. For example, one party should stay in the home with one law enforcement officer while the other party goes outside with other law enforcement; doing this can facilitate honest, transparent statements from each party.

Proper utilization of protocol (such as writing a police report and/or the act of law enforcement separating the victim and the abuser) is *highly* recommended for law enforcement officers to consider and carry out, while completing their investigative interviews involving the victims and perpetrators of domestic abuse.

## Empathy Training

Frequently, victims of domestic abuse reported that law enforcement officers lacked sensitivity and empathetic feelings when responding to a domestic abuse situation. The victims recommended, with regards to working with victims of domestic abuse, that law enforcement is in dire need of sensitivity and empathy training.

During their encounters with law enforcement, victims shared that officers lacked compassion and empathy, as well as an understanding of the abusive dynamic of the victim and abuser. Stacy stated, "They (law enforcement) need to be compassionate and doing what they can in order for you not to feel revictimized." Stacy felt that the treatment that a law enforcement officer shows to a victim is extremely important in navigating the myriad of feelings of the victim. Stacy expressed that it is the duty of law enforcement to be more compassionate, in order to avoid revictimizing when victims are seeking their support.

Many of the victims did feel that revictimization when interacting with law enforcement officers and those officers were not cognizant of the victims' feelings. Anita said:

> Police need sensitivity training. I know that police see people fighting and doing this stuff, and they see this stuff all the time. There are people that don't fight all the time, so when you call for help, they

> should be more sensitive to each person … I found them to be very insensitive in any domestic violence case.

With regards to law enforcement, Anita surmised that officers see these types of calls all the time and they probably feel tired of having to mediate between two conflicting parties. Anita also indicated that based on her experience with law enforcement officers, they could possibly be desensitized to witnessing fighting and arguing that takes place in homes on a regular basis. As a result, there tends to be in some cases, a lack of empathy and sensitivity which can stem from desensitization from addressing domestic abuse calls. For the victims, it may not be a daily occurrence to be engaged in fighting or contentious conflict. From the perspective of many victims, law enforcement tends to be insensitive or not demonstrate empathy … leading the victim to believe this support is completely ineffective.

Maria added that "police don't want to empathize with the victim … police officers do not like the victim because she is causing them headaches because they have to keep coming back." Maria examined the reasons she believed law enforcement do not like dealing with victims of domestic abuse, especially when officers keep coming back to the same residence to make an arrest. She reflected this repetition becomes tiresome and draining for law enforcement officers. However, when law enforcement officers communicate empathetically and compassionately to assist the victim in seeking extensive help, it is a central reason why victims *will follow-up with additional help and support*. The manner in which a law enforcement officer speaks, listens, empathizes and shows compassion towards the victim (while at the scene) creates a feeling of security for the victim. If law enforcement is attempting to help victims of domestic abuse in a compassionate and empathetic manner, then victims deem them to be an effective support.

Jennifer described the treatment of law enforcement when she interacted with them:

> They (law enforcement) bullied me a little bit, and it was awful. I am sure that is not what they intended to do. I think they were trying to pressure me to get help, but it was a real insensitive way that they did it.

It was apparent for Jennifer and for other victims that pressuring or what is perceived as bullying the victim to get help was deemed an ineffective approach for the victim. When law enforcement officers attempt to communicate to the victim about getting help, it cannot be pressured or feel "forced," as it might not benefit the victim's emotional state. Law enforcement officers can make suggestions and offer ideas, but cannot coerce or "force" the victim to do something that she is not emotionally or mentally ready to address. Laura similarly stated:

> They (law enforcement) need kindness training. Their non-verbal expressions floored me. The way they made me feel, like a rug was being pulled beneath me, they could not believe that I was alive. I was still in crisis. There is a more empowering way to speak to an individual and that also shows in their facial expression of shock. They (law enforcement) were shocked and cringed when I told them of my experiences. It did not make me feel good. It made me uncomfortable.

For many victims, it is how law enforcement officers, or any other formal supports *communicate* (either verbally or non-verbally) to the victim that can be extremely disempowering and discouraging. This is especially true when the victim is in active emotional crisis and trauma mode. Not only is it recommended that law enforcement officers assess physical marks and visible crisis, but also for them to receive training in how to communicate and assist effectively with the victim in order to avoid (unintentionally) emotionally revictimizing the victim.

Some victims were surprised when law enforcement officers assisted the abuser more and offered advice to the abuser. Anita stated, "The police were not helpful. They seemed more concerned about his (the abuser's) motorcycle and were questioning him about his bike." Anita relayed that the she was shocked that the police officers that arrived at the scene were collaborating with the abuser and making small talk with him. Again, Anita was in disbelief that the police officers showed more interest in the abuser's motorcycle than her being abused. She expressed that this was extremely unhelpful and ineffective in terms of needing support, help and guidance.

Susan also similarly recalled: "You don't spend half the time helping the abuser and telling them what are his rights." When victims shared that law enforcement officers sided or even bonded with the abuser, their experiences were extremely troubling and contraindicative. It is recommended that law enforcement take statements from both parties and be aware that the abuser is potentially committing the crime and the victim is the individual who is suffering both physically and emotionally. Some victims shared when the abusers had the victims' personal possessions (for example cell phones and other personal belongings), law enforcement officers were also ineffective about returning possessions back to the victim.

Anita shared this of a police interaction during her domestic abuse response call:

> I asked the police to tell him (my husband) to give me back my cell phone and they said: "You are married, it is community property. He can do what he wants." I said, "What do you mean?" The officer said "Since you are married, it is considered community property." Anita responded to the police officer: "So he can destroy everything I own and it is okay?" And he said, "Yes"… plain to my face!

Clearly, Anita and other victims experienced a difficult time in convincing the police officers to get abusers to return victims' possessions. In Anita's case, police officers failed to assist her, in at least convincing the abuser to give back her possessions that he had at the scene.

Maria stated that law enforcement became frustrated with her and her abuser when they were arguing about each other's belongings. Maria shared, "The police said, 'Why can't you guys be grown-ups? Just go over there and get your stuff!'" She also reported that the police officers were frustrated with her and her abuser when it was time to divide up their belongings. In Maria's experiences, she believed the comments, made by law enforcement officers, were belittling and not conducive to being an effective support. As a result of these comments and experiences, Maria felt law enforcement was not on her side and it was difficult to deal with the officers who responded to her situation.

Melissa had similar difficulties with law enforcement officers when it came time to gather and divide her personal belongings. Melissa said:

> I had to let him back into the house to finish getting his stuff. When he got his stuff, he was also taking my stuff and I said, "he cannot take that, that's mine." They (law enforcement) said, "take it up with the judge." It would have been nice if the police officers were on my side.

These approaches (in gathering and dividing personal possessions in a domestic abuse call) from law enforcement officers are not helpful for the victim, who is experiencing the additional victimization of her belongings being taken by the abuser. It is vital for law enforcement officers to develop a more strategic way of having the abuser collect his things … and especially not allowing the abuser to take what *does not belong* to him (as that is another tactic of the abuser victimizing his partner). Law enforcement officers also need to be aware of how traumatic it may be for the victim when the abuser is in the room (even briefly) to gather his belongings. During the separation of belongings from victim and abuser, law enforcement officers need to be present and protective.

Karen reported having a similar experience, as the previously mentioned victims, in interacting with law enforcement while trying to salvage belongings that were important to her. Karen stated, "I did not appreciate not having my cell phone, as the police officer took my cell phone and did not give it back to me." Karen felt similarly to other above victims, with regards to not getting her back her belongings. Discussion of personal belongings may not seem important during a domestic abuse call, but having belongings properly divided (with the assistance of law enforcement) is a first step in assisting and *empowering* a victim in the process of seeking further help. *For domestic abuse victims, proper return of their personal belongings can represent a first step in the restoration of their dignity.*

These victims' statements, and what has been reviewed in this section, reinforces the importance of implementing a type of protocol or procedure of the separation of belongings (of the victim and abuser) highlighted earlier in this chapter. During this separation of belongings, it is critical that law enforcement officers are present and assist (without belittling) the victim. For many victims, this process is very important, since those personal belongings (possessed by the victim) may be the *only* material things that are left for the victims.

Many victims expressed that law enforcement officers communicated with them in an insensitive manner, lacking support and empathy. As a result, empathy training is highly recommended for law enforcement officers in the way that they verbally and non-verbally communicate with domestic abuse victims. Law enforcement officers may find it frustrating in dealing with the victim-population. With the right type of education and training, however, law enforcement officers can gain valuable insight about the level of emotional distortion that takes place between the victim and the abuser. Furthermore, this increase of understanding by law enforcement officers will assist in developing empathy skills when dispatched to a domestic violence call.

Based on the previous information, the following recommendations can be made, with regards to law enforcement:

- The use of standard protocol and procedures for any domestic abuse call.
- Conducting a thorough investigation between victim and abuser.
- Completing a detailed, accurate police report.
- Assisting the victim in gathering or dividing her personal belongings.

In addition, physically separating the two parties is necessary in order for the victim not to fear that her abuser is listening to what she is telling law enforcement officers. This separation also can assist the victims in alleviating anxiety of retaliation from the abuser, because of what they are sharing with law enforcement.

## Low Priority

Some of the victims felt that law enforcement officers perceived domestic abuse calls as "low-priority." The same victims also sensed that the police officers did not want to be at the scene. Karen commented, "It was like, 'we (law enforcement) don't like to get involved in this.'" Maria agreed that she felt that law enforcement view domestic abuse calls as a low priority and that they don't want to be bothered. Maria commented, "The police officers' attitude is like, 'I don't want to be bothered with this; it is low priority.'" Some victims indicated that they felt law enforcement took a low-priority approach so as to discontinue the emotional abuse, which could possibly lead to physical abuse. To Stacy's surprise, the police officers did little (if anything) to eliminate the emotional abuse that took place prior to physical abuse. However, when the abuse became physical, Stacy said, "The officers were remarkable. It was the best circumstance that I had been in; maybe because it was physical … it did not seem like it was a threatening situation until it became physical."

For many law enforcement officers, they may need visual evidence of physical abuse (marks, bruises, scratches, handprints, etc.) in order to make an arrest. It can be extremely difficult to make an arrest based on emotional abuse. However, it is recommended that law enforcement officers attempt to diffuse and de-escalate the level of emotional abuse, which often turns into physical abuse. Stacy stated that she found law enforcement most helpful when the domestic abuse became violent. When domestic abuse becomes physical, victims perceive *at that point* their case becomes high priority, since officers can actually make an arrest.

*The recommendation for law enforcement to provide verbal intervention and de-escalation is important in order to prevent the onset of physical abuse.* By diffusing emotional abuse and making the emotional abuse a high priority, law enforcement is taking a more *proactive* approach, so domestic abuse conflicts do not turn into physical abuse. This proactive approach of addressing and de-escalating emotional abuse can also prevent law enforcement from the repetition of having to go back to the same residence numerous times.

## Referrals/Resources

The importance of referrals and how victims' perceptions of law enforcements view these domestic dispute calls are demonstrated in the second half of this chapter. Law enforcement officers that provide referral and resources to the victims are deemed extremely helpful. It is recommended that law enforcement have resources and referrals when arriving at the scene of a domestic abuse call. Many victims found this to be vital, since they might not have access to such resources or do not know where to go for additional help, support or services. It is recommended that law enforcement officers collate an updated list of resources of other formal supports for victims. This is important for the victim in taking the first steps in seeking further help. Some law enforcement officers even explained the psychological condition that the victims possibly suffered from and offered them resources. These resources were helpful for victims to receive help for physical abuse, such as paramedics, clinics, hospitalization, as well as information and resources of where to seek emotional support. The victims perceived this added support from law enforcement was extremely valuable and necessary in determining their next steps of getting help … and where to go to receive additional formal supports.

Brittany had an abusive boyfriend and she was young when she met her boyfriend. She indicated that her ex-partner was two years older than her and they met at work. In the beginning, their relationship was good.

However, three months into the relationship, her boyfriend became very jealous and possessive. He began to be verbally abusive and eventually became physically abusive. Brittany had to call law enforcement for assistance and she stated, "the police officer gave me the number for a local shelter, the police also gave me a card, but I never called." Even though Brittany did not use the information at the time, she was provided with community referrals, resources and options (which she considered extremely helpful) by the responding officer.

Stacy had a similar experience with law enforcement

> the police officer did go through a list of things that I might need and offered it to me. They gave me a pamphlet of information about domestic abuse and resources offered to victims within my county. Once I read the pamphlet, I was like, "Wow, I am in a domestic abusive situation!"

Stacy was surprised, just by the literature that was given to her from law enforcement officers, to realize she *was* involved in a domestic abuse situation. That pamphlet, given to Stacy by a proactive officer, was *exactly* what she needed to read to finally understand that she was in an abusive relationship.

When victims read about abuse in pamphlets or related literature, they were surprised, but they became aware of the abusive dynamic in their own relationships. The victims were actually experiencing similar scenarios to other victims and they were living in the definition of a domestic abuse relationship. However, victims were unable to *comprehend* this until it was explained to them by either formal or informal supports OR when they read detailed information that was given to them by law enforcement officers. It was not until that point when they realized the type of destructive dynamic of their relationship.

Brittany indicated that law enforcement notified her of a local shelter in the community and that she should go for services: "they handed me a brochure with local shelter and domestic violence information on it. They (law enforcement) told me that I might have 'battered woman syndrome,' and that is when I realized that I might have a problem." Law enforcement can be the first formal support that victims call for assistance. For that reason, law enforcement officers can be that *first step* for the victim, and they can take the time and explain the types of referrals and resources *that will be the next steps* for the victim of domestic abuse. Additionally, the victims reported that knowledge of community resources and identifying what they were experiencing was comforting and eye-opening for them.

It is recommended that law enforcement officers give information and/or resources to the victims, which is deemed highly effective. Providing information to the victims (even if they did not utilize the resources) about seeking additional supports and services started the process in seeking the next steps for the victims. Providing resources and referral information also gave the victims an understanding of the process of how to go about seeking additional help. This is especially important when law enforcement can assist victims in understanding that situation is indeed domestic abuse and against the law. Finally, law enforcement officers can *empower* victims of domestic abuse by sharing that there are resources set in place to assist them in eradicating their abusive relationship.

## Recommendations for Law Enforcement

- The importance of how victims perceived the effectiveness or ineffectiveness of law enforcement officers during a domestic abuse call.
- The gender of the law enforcement officer and an officer's ability to make an emotional connection is significant for the victim.
- The significance of standard protocol and procedures in documentation (and the validity of an accurate and well-written police report).
- The imperative act of separating the victim from the abuser when taking statements, so they are not within earshot of each other.
- The potential impact of empathy and sensitivity training for law enforcement officers.
- The magnitude in understanding of law enforcement learning about the distorted psychological and emotional hold that abusers have over their victim.
- Law enforcement officers receiving education, empathy and sensitivity training will assist in improved treatment and communication with victims in trauma.
- Changing the way law enforcement officers perceived domestic abuse calls as low priority and how some victims felt that law enforcement officers were annoyed or bothered by having to be at the scene of a domestic abuse call.
- Law enforcement officers can be proactive by making an arrest with tangible evidence of a crime being committed, but also attempt to diffuse and de-escalate verbal abuse that might lead to physical abuse (and the repetition of officers returning to the same scene of domestic abuse).
- The importance of having law enforcement officers distribute literature, referrals and resources to the victims of domestic abuse.
- Victims may not understand that they are actually in a domestic abuse situation, until this is explained to them by law enforcement officers (who may be their first point of contact as a formal support).

This chapter gives a significant amount of recommendations (which are continued in following chapters) for formal supports, in interacting or assisting women that are in domestic abuse relationships.

# 3 Mental Health/Social Services

In this chapter, mental health/social services can involve individual/family mental health therapists and social workers, local community mental health centers and shelters. All of these services encompass therapeutic services for victims of domestic abuse. Services may also include case management services, individual, family and group therapy interventions and temporary housing.

Victims discussed the following types of therapeutic interventions:

- Shelters.
- Child therapists.
- Utilizing the internet and research.

Additionally, victims described the effectiveness or ineffectiveness of mental health therapists/social workers and what was the most beneficial for the victim to receive the best outcome and results from this type of formal support.

## Shelters

The first type of therapeutic services addressed is shelters. This formal support not only provides a safe, temporary living arrangement for the victims and their children, but also gives victims wraparound services, which can include group and individual sessions. In this environment/setting, victims' responses of the assistance that they received from shelters ranged from negative-to-non-existent to positive. Historically, domestic violence shelters did not open their doors until the early 1970s, and there were more shelters for animals than for abused women. Times have changed and progressively there have been movements and laws put into place for the safety of women and their children. However, there is still a tremendous need for the existence and availability of shelters for victims of domestic abuse and their families. The effectiveness of shelters varied from victim to victim when they explained their experiences within this formal support system.

Natasha stated that the other victims at the domestic violence shelter seemed to be territorial:

> We went to a crisis shelter. We got there, did an intake, and we were gone for an hour, and took all our stuff and did not stay there. It was territorial inside the crisis center itself; it was predominantly negative. It felt like that people were in there just parked there in the shelter and not necessarily a refuge. The shelter was territorial, they (victims) had everything staked out, the room and the TV. The staff at the shelter seemed drained … like no energy. The security was poor; they had a security guard who was sleeping on the job and he was pretty new. The residents seemed territorial and like; "This is my space. Good luck trying to find a place to sit." They were not very nice. The crisis shelter was so uninviting, so institutionalized and I felt that we had a bigger problem because we did not escape earlier and we were scared. We were scared of that feeling of not being safe. Our things were stolen by people, and the victims were angry and it felt like there was going to be altercations and conflict.

Natasha's experience at the local shelter was negative. She felt that the other victims there were oppositional and confrontational, as well as territorial of the space in the shelter. According to Natasha, the shelter staff was limited and the staff there did not seem to interact or engage with the victims. Natasha felt that if she had stayed, she would have gotten into an altercation with another victim and she felt uncomfortable. Natasha reiterated that the environment was uninviting with limited staff and rules. The recommendation for shelters is to maintain full capacity with the *sufficient amount of properly trained staff*, in order to set a supportive climate and tone of the shelter. As a result, the shelter will not be viewed as a contentious or quarrelsome environment for victims. It is also important for all victims to *understand the ground rules of the shelter* and for shelter employees to fully explain these rules to them. Shelter employees need to be fully available for the victims to help them get acclimated to their new environment.

Cindy discussed her needs at the shelter, "The shelter that I went to, I wanted more education and information, but they were talking about vague things." Cindy reported that her experiences at the shelter were not educational and did not provide information regarding domestic abuse. Cindy needed more information about domestic abuse at the shelter, particularly knowing that it was only a temporary stay. Cindy wanted more details of what she was experiencing instead of vague, shallow dialogues. It is recommended that shelters have *ample, up-to-date information, literature and wraparound individual and group sessions led by properly trained staff members*, in order for victims to fully understand the dynamics of domestic abuse and their experiences.

Anita said that she could not attend any of the therapeutic groups or individual sessions:

> The shelter had different interventions for me to participate in. They had a system if I stayed. However, I was working and enrolled in college. It was difficult for me to participate in their interventions because of the things that I had going on. I was working and never got the opportunity to participate in the vast amount of resources because I still had to work. So, I did not receive counseling at the shelter.

Anita reported that her experiences at the shelter, as well as her obligations to work and school, were her priority for survival. As a result, she did not/could not participate in any of the therapeutic services and supports at the shelter. Many shelters have programs that provide therapeutic services and tools based around the victim's individual schedule (for example, if the victim is attending school or working). This reinforces that shelters should adhere to what was discussed in Part 1 – in Seeking Help: "No One-Size-Fits-All Solution." It is recommended that while victims are at the shelter and offered support, they should also be provided with *individualized services and customized supports that fit into the victims' schedules*. Anita stated that the shelter provided her a place for respite and safety, but it did not provide any counseling or case management in order for her to become more *empowered* and *independent* of her abuser and not let domestic abuse be a recurring problem for her.

Some victims gained knowledge and insight from the shelter services and this was deemed important for the victims (during their shelter stay). Cindy described that the counselors at the shelter reassured her that she needed to be at the shelter and that she was, in fact, being abused. Cindy revealed, "I told the counselor my story and she said that I am being abused and you can get help here." Cindy felt reassurance, validation and confirmation that she was in the right place for her and she belonged at the shelter. Some victims felt that the groups at the shelter were very beneficial to them and assisted them in making sense of their abusive dynamic. For example, Melissa summarized her experience of the wrap-around services available to her:

> The services (at the shelter) were beneficial. They made me set up a "safety plan" on the very next day that I signed up for group and individual counseling. I registered for all types of programming at the shelter. I signed up for parenting classes, anger management and a crisis group to start up with. The crisis group was a four-week overview of all the services at the shelter, red flags to look for in a relationship and what an unhealthy relationship looks like … just reiterating the safety plan and an overall view of what I needed to know while I was there. The parenting course that I took reinforced

> good behavior, modifying bad behavior, keeping me on track with trying to have a steady bed time, and what the kids need to grow up healthy … just to be healthy myself. The anger management groups were the most helpful. I learned how to diffuse the situation and to calm myself down, as well as not allow a situation to escalate. This would become detrimental and allows you to get angered. It is how you handle the anger and deal with the anger that is the most important. The group helped me to deal with lingering effects, different relaxation techniques, why I feel the way I do and different triggers. It helps to know what you are thinking before. The self-esteem group was more of a motivational group; how to better ourselves and how to plan and reach goals that we have set, and most importantly how to take care of ourselves.

Melissa was offered different groups from self-esteem and anger management to parenting her children. These groups and services helped her to gain information, knowledge and education of these important useful topics that were relevant to her at that time. Melissa and other victims were able to illustrate how the groups had helped them in order for her to make the necessary, systemic changes within themselves and their lives. Some women who suffered from domestic abuse felt that the shelter was effective and viewed the services and supports as necessary to inform them of the seriousness of their abusive relationships. Laura expressed that the local shelter, "helped me with every group I needed. I was listening to the groups and listening to women's stories, it had nothing to do with looks, color, nationality, or education." Laura recalled that everyone looked physically different, but internally it was apparent that they had all went through similar experiences. Laura grasped more of an understanding of her situation as she would listen to other women tell their stories.

Maria recalled her experience at the shelter as being effective because of the amount of wraparound services in which she had available. Maria recalled:

> They did an intake on me which was awesome. A lot of people who work there know what you are talking about, she (shelter staff) told me, "I had been a victim and an abuser." The intake takes about two hours, you have to sign a lot of stuff, you are never going to tell where it is, who is there, and they shock you to realize how serious it really is because you are in such a haze. I told her (shelter staff) about how I tried to break up with him and she stopped me and she said, "What do you think is love? This is not love. That is crazy; he stalked you. You realize that, right?" They give you food and a place to stay. They talk to you and have groups, which were good to hear other people's stories.

Many of the victims, who utilized shelters as a form of support, felt that if the staff experienced domestic abuse themselves, then those staff knew the emotional trauma and disruption that the victims had experienced. Furthermore, the shelter staff who had previously experienced abuse or knew how it felt to be victimized could *empathize better with the victims*. According to the victims, when shelter staff were interacting with the victims, they were "educating them back in reality". The support groups were helpful for the women to tell their stories and learn from others, especially about the types of abuse, their feelings within the dynamic and their feelings in the here-and-now. Many victims did not know or had never experienced unconditional love and support. As a result, learning about unconditional love was new and shifted the paradigm about what victims perceived as healthy versus unhealthy relationships. Victims who experienced support from shelters had varied feedback.

The following are recommendations for shelters that serve victims of domestic abuse:

- Provide rules and regulations about the shelter and set the level of expectations of the shelter for the victim.
- Customize times and schedules in which *ALL* victims are receiving not only housing and food, but also education, information, sessions (group/individual).
- Provide a variety of topics for group and individual sessions that are used as tools and techniques in which the victims can learn and implement.
- Have adequate staffing at the shelter, in order for victims to get the most support and services.
- Staff members at the shelter need to be ready, rested and accessible to victims and not appear to be burnt-out, exhausted or drained.
- Shelter staff need to set a positive tone for victims rather than condoning a contentious atmosphere, where the victim is not again in fear and retraumatized or feels threatened by other victims.
- Shelter staff members and security must understand and be vigilant of the victims' overall physical and emotional safety, both in and out of the shelter.

## Child Therapists

Some victims noted that they thought the therapists working with their children were surprisingly helpful and beneficial to both their children and to themselves. Karen explained that the therapist working with her child noted red flags for how her son was interacting with other children. Karen stated, "My son has a lot of tendencies and red flags. They were trying to get him to interact and let him know when he is being inappropriate." The child therapist identified some concerns about Karen's child and how to reinforce more appropriate interactions with his peers. Victims, who were interacting with child therapists, were thankful when the therapists also assisted them with the overall process of protecting victims and their families. Denise shared, "The therapist helped me out with my children and informed me of getting a restraining order, as well as the overall process." Denise implemented the recommendation of the child's therapist in considering and obtaining a restraining order against her abuser.

Stacy also identified the therapist working with her children as, "being extremely effective with a team that came to the house to describe wraparound services (for her and her children). With formal supports and having someone come to the house and explain the services was comforting and definitely helpful." Stacy also discussed that knowing there were formal supports, such as therapists for herself and for her children and wraparound services made her feel *very supported and optimistic about seeking help for herself and for her children.*

A child therapist told Melissa that she was concerned about the interactions between her and her abuser. The victim noted that the child therapist observed both the abuser and victim in the waiting room. Melissa shared:

> My daughter's counselor observed how he (the abuser) acted toward me, and she ended up calling me in and saying "I don't feel comfortable with how he is with you … and here is why." She put into words what I had been feeling. The child therapist reported, "I think it is a dangerous situation that you are in, and you need to consider getting out of it."

Even though this was her daughter's counselor, Melissa realized that she was able to make a concise observation to her and this validated Melissa's feelings. The child therapist was transparent and honest with Melissa, based on her observations of how Melissa and her abuser were behaving while in her presence. Her child's therapist also expressed her concern about Melissa and her daughter being in a dangerous situation. The child's therapist made observations and notations based on the child's behavior and the way Melissa and her abuser were interacting with each other in the waiting room.

Many victims expressed much gratitude for the help the child therapist provided for their children and for themselves. The child therapists succeeded in assisting the victims and offering support and encouragement for the victims and their children.

The child therapists also *explained how a family was in an unhealthy dynamic with an abuser and how that affected the family as a whole.*

The following are recommendations for child therapists working with domestic abuse victims and their children:

- Recognize the warning signs and "red flags" of the victim's child's behavior and understand how to assist in modifying behavior to be more socially appropriate for the child.
- To have the child therapist be open and transparent about what he/she is witnessing within the dynamic of the victim and abuser.
- When therapists make observations of maladaptive behaviors within the abusive dynamic, they should highlight character flaws, maladaptive traits or questionable behaviors of the abuser. The victim may be aware these flaws, traits or behaviors, however, the victim may not report this to anyone. Having a child therapist communicating these points to the victim can raise more awareness in helping her to see some simple character traits and tension between the abuser and victim.
- A child therapist can not only discuss progress with the victims, but also give suggestions of steps needed in order to stay protected and safe from harm.

## Internet Counseling and Blogging

With the rapid advancement of technology, many victims turn to a non-traditional form of counseling – internet counseling. This includes: Skyping with therapists in sessions and utilizing the internet as a form of bibliotherapy and research as a vital form of self-help. It was reported by the victims that when they could identify what was specifically wrong, then they wanted to learn more about it. As a result, many victims did their own researching on databases and websites to learn if they could to relate to others' experiences or situations – those similar to what was occurring in their own homes. Several victims learned more about common character traits of a "typical" abuser. Some victims began blogging, writing their experiences and soliciting feedback from other victims and/or participants in the forum. Other victims did not feel comfortable with sharing, however they immersed themselves in reading similar traumatic experiences that other victims were living or had lived. Many of the victims felt comforted by the fact that *they were not alone* in the struggle and they felt reassurance and validation from these messages and forums. They even acknowledged that a form of education (and gained insight) had occurred. Some victims participated in electronic counseling via Skyping.

Susan commented how on effective internet counseling was when she interacted with other victims and stated:

> I received internet counseling as it was recommended that I get other, additional local help. The internet counseling made me face what I was able to process in the beginning for me. I did not feel alone with the internet counseling services, it was necessary to seek out counseling when I did and the way I did.

Some victims are physically trapped and cannot leave the house (because of their abusers' entrapment), so victims have to become "creative" in getting the necessary help for themselves. As a result, some victims did their own independent research and communicated on online forums, which was an encouraging start to gain understanding and strive for emotional progress. Susan noted that having the internet resources and doing the research online was a gateway to seeking additional therapeutic services. She stressed that she was able to process her feelings, as she did not feel alone when she did decide to reach out. Doing this made Susan want to reach out *become more empowered* and validated her need to continue her independent work and self-discovery.

Through reading and participation in online blogs and groups, Cindy was able to educate herself in relating to other victims' struggles and experiences. This made her fully aware and cognizant of the abuse she had endured. Cindy responded, "I did not type anything in. I mainly just read. I just wanted to educate myself as to the realization for me, that I was being abused." Cindy felt seeking answers and doing her own research on the internet, in addition to the online chats that she was reading, was very beneficial for her. Anita also blogged on the internet and wrote to an author of a book she was reading about domestic violence. Anita stated, "I wrote a blog about it. I wrote this whole story and I was getting it off my chest. I tried to stay proactive and positive." Anita expressed that blogging and reaching out to the author of the domestic violence book helped her process her own story and promoted positivity in her life. Natasha said, "I was doing research and reading on everything that I could. I realized that the online site was a forum. I started reading in the beginning and then started to write my own stuff, which was very helpful." Natasha asked questions to victims online, they replied and they also referred her to other related sites that provided her additional information. Cindy felt that by doing her own investigative work and bibliotherapy on her own solidified it for her: "reading it really brought it to life; hearing it did not do it for me."

This type of intervention is an important recommendation for victims to initiate their own journeys of self-discovery and self-awareness through reading, inquiring and blogging about their own lives. Here are some recommendations for victims to seek out non-traditional supports:

- Independent reading, researching and learning online.
- Sharing and expressing in an online forum was reported to be quite helpful for many of the victims, who suffered emotional, physical or sexual abuse.
- Finding safe and supportive online groups allowed victims to be in a community of women (with similar experiences) and reading similar experiences from other victims was enlightening and educational.

- Some victims preferred not to be instructed, but rather initiated their own developed style of independently receiving formal supports online, group chats, bibliography and research. Doing this was considered helpful and insightful to the victims who engaged in these type of interventions.

The second half of Chapter 3 will reveal the types of counseling services that are both needed and wanted by the victims. This section is intended for counselors, therapists, social services agencies, private practice clinicians and community mental health agencies. It will describe what victims believed was helpful and what was not helpful when providing additional formal supports. In this section, the following will be highlighted:

- Education and Specialization.
- Effective Character Traits in Clinicians.
- Challenging Beliefs.
- Processing Victims' Stories.

## Education and Specialization

The amount of formal education and specific experience of a professional who is assisting domestic abuse victims was perceived as extremely important to the victims. In addition, the education and specialization of therapists were viewed as critical components in the benefit of seeking professional services. Monique felt that the education of her therapist was important enough to note, "I had a therapist who had a Ph.D. in psychology." Monique's therapist having a Ph.D. was significant to Monique because she felt reassured in her therapist having the highest level of formal education. For Monique and many other victims, this high level of formal education and specialized experience indicated that the therapist had more knowledgeable and had better insight into domestic abuse (as opposed to a professional with a bachelor's level/undergraduate degree). Victims perceived a therapist with a high level of education, specializing in domestic abuse as important, in order to receive the best support and reassurance in rebuilding their lives.

Katie emphasized that her therapist was an intern and that she did not know that fact until she asked how long she had been working at the center. When her therapist told her that she had two weeks' experience and that she was an intern, Katie was very disappointed and became discouraged because she did not feel that she was going to get quality of services. Katie said:

> She (the counselor) was an intern and I did not know she was an intern from the beginning. I figured it out because I had asked her how long she has been working at the center. She told me she had only been working there for two weeks. I went away very discouraged.

Prior to her asking, Katie could tell that her therapist was not experienced nor had specialized long enough to help her effectively. It is important for therapists to be trained and to have the education, knowledge and specialization to assist the victim population. In addition to having the educational credentials, it is imperative for victims to know that their therapists truly specialize in domestic abuse. Maria compared therapists that had experience in hearing about abuse and violence versus other therapists that dealt with less intense topics.

Maria explained it this way:

> I called a private practice with 16 to 20 therapists, I said, "I want a therapist that has dealt with domestic violence. I have lived in a shelter. I want someone who can handle it and knows what the hell I am talking about. I don't want a therapist who is used to dealing with rich bitches and Xanax who say 'Oh my husband does not pay attention to me.'" Whoopee, that is a different type of therapist. She called me up and goes, "I want to talk to you" because I said, "Have you ever dealt with this?" She (therapist) said, "I used to work in a battered women's shelter," I said, "Really?" And she said, "Yeah, I deal with them (victims before they leave, while they are there and after they leave)." That is what I am talking about. I wanted to tell her some really, really horrible stuff that he was doing to me before I left that I could not tell the other therapist. I needed to tell someone because it was so horrible. I told her and I felt so much better. Not everyone (therapists) can deal with this. I told her, "I need you to make me strong." You have to feel strong again; that is why I went to this therapist.

Maria needed to share her abuse with an experienced and specialized therapist who was able to digest her story and not feel uncomfortable with the level of severity of violence and abuse that Maria endured while in the relationship. The amount of schooling and experience of the therapist is important for the victim, in order to feel reassured about the quality of services and support she is seeking from that clinician.

## Effective Character Traits in Clinicians

Several of the victims switched therapists, due to their first therapist being overall too passive, soft spoken and not challenging their distorted cognitions or perceptions. Natasha identified that her therapist,

> was helpful because she validated me, but not helpful because she did not give me other perspectives or challenge me. The first therapist I saw was passive; she was very low-key, very soft voice and slow

> speech. I would tell her what had happened during the week and be such a wreck, maybe she saw I was in denial.

Natasha identified the difference in approaches by her two therapists and she concluded that her first therapist was not effective enough due by being too passive and an overall feeling of "Yes, ma'am" to the victim. Natasha found the therapist's personality traits of being low-key, soft spoken, passive, with slow speech and not challenging her beliefs ineffective when it came to receiving therapeutic services and support. Natasha switched therapists and then compared her new therapist to her previous one:

> She gave me a lot of work to think about what I needed to do for the next session and to make a list of stuff I needed to do. She was challenging me on what I was saying and the therapist asked me, "Don't you think you are reacting this way because of this?"

Natasha described ways that her new therapist was able to talk to her. For example, the therapist reviewed Natasha's symptoms and she was very thorough, challenging and confronting Natasha's belief system in an empathetic manner. She also shared that her new therapist would always leave her with something to think about and what to work on outside of the therapy session, such as homework and making a list of things to do for the next session. Utilizing this therapeutic approach can assist the victim of continued progress in a forward direction with each therapeutic session.

In a similar conversation, Monique described her and her abuser's experience in marital counseling with the therapist, "The therapist was passive. He did give us tools though to get through it, and it was helpful up to a point." Monique also concluded that the tools that the therapist gave them were helpful but Monique considered the therapist as being too passive and ineffective in a therapeutic setting.

## Challenging Beliefs

Victims of domestic abuse viewed that the most effective type of counseling occurred when the therapist challenged the victim in an empathetic manner. Therapists, who challenged the victim to think about their own distortions, were considered significantly effective by the victims. Cindy received individual therapy, but did not think the therapist's techniques were effective, "The therapist guided me through exercises versus telling me or helping me. I needed to be more informed rather than do exercises, I learn from work versus a game." Cindy believed that learning from an exercise or lesson technique was ineffective and she expressed that she wanted her beliefs to be challenged in more, direct way. Brittany reported that the effectiveness of her therapist was due to her challenging Brittany to think within the therapeutic process. Brittany articulated,

> She (her therapist) made me think a lot. She asked questions and it made me think. Every time I left there, I would think about it what she would say and think "Okay, I understand that or I don't understand that." It took me a long time.

Brittany liked the fact that she was getting challenged and she always left with something to think about for the following session. Brittany's therapist asked her questions pertaining to her experience with her abuser and *this resulted in thinking from a different perspective.*

## Processing Victims' Stories

It is important to allow the victim to process their story. Several victims felt that it was helpful when social services or mental health professionals allowed them to share and process their story in its entirety. Some victims felt it helpful if they were urged to disclose their experiences. Furthermore, victims who shared their stories believed a significant part of the healing process was continuing to seek and receive help.

Susan reported that, "getting help is helping me. They make me talk about it." Susan found it effective when she was permitted to process her victimization and explain her story in the act of getting help. Stacy considered it helpful when her therapist was able to reflectively listen to her. Stacy noted that when the therapist utilized reflective listening or reframing, it made her understand what type of situation she was in and she stated:

> counseling for me was good. Just letting myself talk to get where I should be. "Do you think this works for you?" She (the therapist) summarized everything that I told her and then hearing it, it was like "Wow! This is not a good situation!".

Stacy found it helpful and effective that her therapist summarized, reframed and reflected during her therapeutic sessions. Stacy's therapist was able to take what she said and by using her own words and phrases, summarized by reframing Stacy's story. Reframing is a technique that is oftentimes used during counseling sessions by a trained, mental health professionals and *reframing is particularly effective when working with victims of domestic abuse.*

It is important for therapists to provide an ample amount of time for the victim to process and share her story and for the therapist not to progress right into solution-focused or problem-solving mode. The victims found that many of their therapists were more interested in having them leave their abuser when the victims did not feel psychologically ready. The victims wanted to share their stories and felt that many of the therapists were not as interested in processing the abuse. This is known as transference. Transference is when therapists project their own issues onto the victim. This is extremely counterproductive for the victim.

Melissa reported:

> I had never spoken about it, and I appreciated being able to talk about it. I felt the more I came in to talk about it, and I could not do anything about my situation at the time. For me, it was a huge step going in and talking about it. I felt like they were like, "Okay, so what else are you here for?" The counselor never said that to me. I felt like I was going in and complaining about the situation; they would tell me how to get out of it, which I understand is valid. I just did not feel connected. However, I wanted to tell my story. I did not want to get out of it; telling it was so new to me and such a big process. This is all I wanted to do and actually admitting that this is my life and this is my story.

Melissa had never discussed or processed her domestic abuse with anyone. The act of Melissa coming into a therapeutic session, to discuss her abusive situation, was *monumental* for her. However, her counseling sessions were unhelpful, due to the fact that she was unable to relate to the therapist. Melissa's therapist immediately became solution-focused, while Melissa wanted to share her story for the first time.

Monique also needed to process her story without interruption. However, the therapist tried to get her to focus on anything but her story, such as leaving her abuser. *Processing the story for the victim is a necessity.*

Monique reported:

> I needed to figure out how to process my story. I did not know how to channel my energy into expressing it vocally or any other way. That was important for me and I never got that need met. Each week when I went in with other issues, she (therapist) would say, "Here we go again, and you're in the story." For me processing my story was helpful. I had to switch counselors.

Monique felt as though she was not getting her needs met on a therapeutic level, since she was not given the opportunity to process her abuse with the counselor. For many victims, being able to process their stories is paramount, since they could not share their stories with anyone, particularly a professional, as demonstrated earlier in Part 1 with "Seeking Help". Many victims felt it was ineffective when the therapist did not allow them to be open and stay in their story for a while. According to some victims, therapists were too quick to get to solution-focused and problem-solving techniques (prior to the victim being psychologically ready). It was also not beneficial when therapists pushed their own philosophies and views onto the victims, prior to processing their stories in their entirety. This transference of therapists projecting onto the victims stems from the therapist and victim not being at the same point of understanding.

The main goals of Chapter 3 are to assist social services and mental health professionals in formal supports and services that were both effective and ineffective for the victims. This chapter highlighted shelters, child therapists and the utilization and benefits of online forums, online counseling and internet research. This chapter also explained what was helpful and not helpful, involving therapeutic sessions and the type of therapist best suited in assisting victims. In summary, mental health professionals need to be educated specialists in dealing with the domestic abuse victim population. Therapists ought not to be passive, but instead empathetic and direct in giving information to the victim. It is also advantageous for the therapist by challenging victims' belief systems, yet also allowing victims to entirely process their stories.

# 4 Medical Staff and Clergy

Medical staff and personnel are comprised of medical doctors, nurses and hospital staff. Interviewed victims would only have contemplated going to a doctor or medical office if they thought their injuries were significant. Many victims viewed their interactions with medical staff at the doctors or hospitals as being ineffective, as evidenced by the following:

- Victims' belief that medical professionals were unable to relate to them.
- Confidentiality and HIPAA violations.
- Not conducting a thorough assessment and evaluation of the victim.

Previous research in a medical setting suggested that with repeated violence or continued trauma, there will be more medical and psychiatric symptoms. The injuries that the victims incur may require hospitalization and intense medical treatment. Many of these victims will go on to have continued episodes of violence and repeated incidents of violence and injuries. It is important that medical practitioners make note of these peculiar injuries and possibly verbally assess the victim to see about how the injuries came to be and other markings that she has endured.

## Victims' Belief that Medical Professionals were Unable to Relate to Them

Victims shared that when they *did* disclose the abuse to medical staff, they perceived the dialogue shifted into a lecture. This shift in tone made it very uncomfortable for the victim to think about disclosing additional information. Furthermore, this made it challenging for the victim to further describe her abuse and rationale for her injuries. As a result, the victims felt that the medical professionals were *not able to relate* to their trauma.

Melissa shared her experience:

> at the hospital, there were many of times when I should have gone. I did what I had to do. They tried get me to share his identity. They wanted to bring the cops there; they could not do that without me agreeing to it. They did let it go when I wouldn't – they did treat me. The second time I went to the doctor, the doctor's nurse was cold and she was giving me a lot of lecturing.

When victims of domestic abuse were seeking help or taking steps to leave their violent environment, they considered it contraindicative to listen to lecturers or experience a professional "talking down to them." In Melissa's case, she needed support and medical attention. Conversely, Anita identified the effectiveness of support and medical services, when she spoke with her doctor and her doctor was able to relate to her. This was reinforced when Anita's symptoms were documented and a medical examination occurred. Anita also expressed that she felt validated when her doctor reassured her and spoke with her about the psychological components of her situation during her visit.

Anita recalled:

> He (medical doctor) recommended that I keep blogging and I was keeping a journal of my thoughts. He said that "you are going to be fine." I went there (doctor's appointment) because I could not breathe, as it was stress-induced. He said, "Your breathing is fine," and I am like, "I am not." I could not breathe. I told him (doctor) that I left my husband and I got a restraining order for domestic violence. He said, "Don't worry about it; you are going to be fine."

Anita felt she was comfortable enough to have an honest dialogue and open communication with her medical provider because she felt that her doctor was able to reassure, communicate and listen to her. Anita's doctor was also able to provide her with recommendations to address her concerns that were psychological symptoms rather than a medical condition. She needed to feel validated and reassured at that time. Often, victims may not have any physical complaints or injuries, but they may present with psychological symptoms from the abuse that interferes with their level of functioning. It is *imperative* that medical professionals listen openly to the victim, who expresses these psychological complaints based on the disclosed abuse. It is also vital for medical practitioners to understand that a bigger issue may be causing such distress for the patient. It may also be necessary for the medical doctor to provide a referral to a psychiatrist in order to more appropriately deal with the victim's potential mental health diagnoses and behavioral changes.

*It is NOT recommended for medical practitioners or other formal supports to refer the victim to family therapy.* This type of referral is contradictive and places the victim in a more heightened state of victimization, as well as endangering her safety. From the victim's perspective, if she receives a referral to family therapy, it is perceived that the domestic abuse is not being recognized as a crime or that (the abuser) breaking the law is not being taken seriously. This can trigger an increase in the victim's fears and anxieties with the thought of interacting with the abuser.

## Victim Safety

It is important that both medical practitioners and mental health clinicians formulate a safety plan with the victim in order to keep her safe and protected. A doctor or medical professional can address this by asking questions such as:

- Do you want to go back to your partner at this time and have a follow-up appointment?
- Do you fear for your life?
- What have you done legally in order to stay protected?
- Who can support you through this critical time?
- Is there someone you can reside with that you feel comfortable within a temporary living situation?
- Do you have access to your own money?
- What safety measures do you have in place in the home, so no one can break in such as cameras, lock changes and/or secured windows?

These are just some examples of questions that any doctor or medical practitioner should ask in keeping the patient safe and protected. Often, medical practitioners may feel that they are not equipped to deal with such intense familial or psychological issues, and or even "blame" the victim for provocation. Medical practitioners may also feel like it is "not their place" to investigate so deeply into abuse issues or they may feel like the victim's trauma is out of their scope of practice. As a result of this rationale, women who are being abused will continue to go undetected and overlooked from a medical standpoint.

## Pregnant Victims

Medical practitioners and personnel need to be *especially* vigilant that emotional and physical violence has a tendency to increase when the patient is pregnant. This can be a result of the victim's focal point not solely being on the abuser and the abuser not liking having to share the attention with their unborn child. Victims that are pregnant tend to be more physically vulnerable, hence more of a reason for the abuser to increase the level of severity of abuse onto the victim. Medical practitioners can recognize when examining a pregnant patient if she has been involved in an abusive dynamic by the location of her injuries, substance abuse addiction or dependency or frequent usage and lack or delayed prenatal care, lack of nutrition and abnormal or excessive pain during the pregnancy.

Even more alarming is the increased frequency of abuse and the severity of abuse that can take place when the victim is pregnant, putting both the victim and unborn child in harm's way. Abusers tend to have specific character traits when interacting with the victim: being controlling, accusatory and blaming the victim, intimidating the victim and instilling a high intensity of fear in her, name-calling, degrading and demeaning treatment, jealousy and possessiveness, erratic behavior that is risky, reckless and dangerous acts, creating uneasiness in the victim, manipulation, "Dr. Jekyll/Mr. Hyde" personality trait (this is when the abuser is kind and loving, and in a split second will become aggressive and enraged).

## Confidentiality and HIPAA Violations

Laura described that she and her abuser were both talking to the nurse at the same time and in the same examination room. Laura said,

> The nurse said to me, in front of him (the abuser), "Have you been abused?" He said in a joking manner, "Of course, I beat her all the time!" The nurse started to laugh hysterically and they (the abuser and nurse) were both laughing together.

For Laura, this experience was so *psychologically damaging and disrespectful* because she actually was getting abused and the nurse did not take into consideration to not to ask any related abuse questions in front of her abuser. Hence, this can be a reason why many victims feel that medical staff do not take their statements in a confidential manner or seriously consider what the victim is sharing with them. Laura felt *defeated* that the abuser and nurse made a joke out of her abusive situation. Laura also was particularly upset that her abuser was in the room while she was being questioned, as this did not allow for Laura or other victims to share openly and honestly about what was really occurring. This lack of confidentiality is a critical violation of HIPAA regulations and violates the ability to keep the victim's statements private. Nursing staff and doctors have a patient/doctor confidentiality obligation *and* an obligation to report to law enforcement (as an added component of the HIPAA law) if the victim is abused based on the injuries and that a criminal act has occurred. Additionally, many hospitals and hospital personnel do not want to break confidentiality of a victim for fear of them never seeking help again. When a victim may be presenting with abusive marks and there are clear signs of abuse, it is recommended to seek out a referral from a hospital social worker or hospital psychiatrist to further evaluate and assess the patient. Unfortunately, in the medical environment, completing a thorough assessment, including asking specific questions about abuse, does not often occur.

There are many instances when a victim needs to go to hospital but the abuser knows that he will get in trouble with the law. Therefore, the abuser will prevent the victim from seeking necessary medical attention. Some victims are forced by their abusers to come into the examination room (with their abusers). *This is done to clearly make a point to be present while the victim makes her statements about her injuries to the nursing staff and/or doctor, in order for her abuser not to get in trouble with the law.* This is not only unhelpful, but also *extremely* dangerous for the victim, as it also violates the victim's confidentiality and basic HIPAA laws.

It is important to note that HIPAA guidelines do not prevent law enforcement from obtaining certain medical records that relate to criminal activity. Hospital staff and medical practitioners should not prevent accessibility to a patient who is a wounded and who is a victim of a crime. It is important and recommended that medical practitioners become more familiar with the legalities and responsibilities when coming in contact with women who are abused and seeking medical attention. Sadly, the discouraging fact is there continues to be cases where the hospital (or medical staff)*break the victim's confidentiality right in front of her abuser.* Having the abuser present, when the victim is being questioned or examined by medical personnel actually happens more often than realized, and it is completely *unacceptable* and *dangerous* for the victim. When the abuser is present during medical questioning, the abuser continues to exert power and control over the victim.

It is recommended that medical doctors and trained personnel see *only* the identified patient alone, unless that patient is deemed incompetent (and then having another representative present, besides the abuser). This is to *prevent* the abuser from escorting the victim, monitoring what she informs medical staff and protecting him from getting in trouble with the law.

An example of this is described by Melissa, who had a situation where the doctor allowed her abuser to sit in on the medical examination. She recalled, "I was unable to discuss anything about the relationship with the doctor, because he (abuser) insisted on being in all of my appointments with me. The doctor allowed for him to sit while I was being examined." Both Melissa and Laura felt that their confidentiality was *violated*, due to both doctors and medical staff not giving them their *privacy* by having their medical examinations performed with their abusers present.

## Not Conducting a Thorough Assessment and Evaluation of the Victim

There is a misconception that an assessment, used to determine if domestic abuse is occurring, is a matter of a few questions that nurses or medical staff ask the victim while waiting in the examination room. There needs to be a *comprehensive and effective evaluation* or *a specific assessment with more involved questions* relating to any type of abuse. Having a comprehensive, effective evaluation or assessment, conducted by trained medical personnel will help to determine if domestic abuse is occurring in the victim's life related to her presenting medical injuries, especially if the victim has repetitive visits for injuries that could have been caused by the abuser. Due to their feelings of embarrassment or humiliation, victims may often *avoid being truthful or completely not disclose information* about their injuries. Additionally, many victims *fear retaliation* if they are completely transparent with the medical staff about how they obtained their injuries. Victims are also anxious from the fear of a written police report (that is compiled by law enforcement with information from medical practitioner) to arrest the abuser due to the medical evaluation and responses by the victim. A medical practitioner may assume that the victim is being abused, however, the victim may not disclose in full because she is not *psychologically ready*, and the medical practitioner must consider this when evaluating a patient who presents with symptoms of abuse. Unfortunately, there can be many instances when medical practitioners overlook domestic abuse as a source of medical injuries or psychological symptoms, due to lack of a thorough assessment or an evaluation not being completed.

Listed are some useful, suggested medical assessments and models (to evaluate if a victim is in danger and if her safety is at risk) for medical practitioners to implement within their practice of treatment. The screening tool "HITS" is a four-item tool that asks the victim if she is in danger and the type of abuse that is endured. This tool has a Likert scale from 1 (never occurring) to 5 (frequently occurring); 10 or more signifies that there is domestic abuse happening in the home. "WAST-SF (Women Abuse Screening Tool – Short Form)", is a screening tool, but is more of a clinical evaluation. This tool describes the intimate partner relationship and how conflicts escalate. There is no type of scoring with this tool, it is more of an evaluation. Another screening tool that medical practitioners can use is called "Partner Violence Screen", which is a three-item questionnaire asking whether or not the patient feels safe in her currently living situation. "The Relationship Chart" is another screening tool which can be administered to female patients suspected of enduring domestic abuse, it consists of four items of the level and frequency of emotional and physical abuse. Another screening tool is the "Computer-Based IPV Questionnaire", which is self-administrated. It mainly assesses safety to reflect whether or not the patient is being abused emotionally and/or physically. These suggested screening tools and evaluations provide more thorough and detailed responses from victims being seen in a hospital setting or within medical practices. Many medical practitioners do not have the tools in which to determine if abuse is occurring, even if they are suspicious of it. These above listed assessments can provide *red flags* for practitioners to the types of injuries that may be occurring and if the injury has been inflicted by another individual, particularly if the visits are multiple or repetitive.

Medical practitioners can determine physical symptoms of abuse such as defensive injuries in exposed areas such as the face, arms and legs. Many pregnant women have differing signs of abuse that occur in the chest, stomach area, reproductive organs and anus. Other indicators include psychosomatic illnesses, repeated injuries, psychological symptoms and behavioral changes, altered sleeping and/or eating patterns, suicidal ideations or intent and/or submissive non-verbal communication such as no eye contact, delayed and soft-spoken responses.

There are also signs of domestic abuse that medical practitioners can look for to identify if abuse is occurring with their patient while the abuser is escorting her to the appointment. As previously stated, it is important for abusers not to be present in the examination room. A medical practitioner can be vigilant of the abuser by observing the following: irrational behavior, jealousy and possessiveness, ability to control the amount of time the victims spends with the healthcare professional, abusers talking over the victim and/or communicating for her to the staff.

If medical practitioners have a suspicion that abuse is occurring with a patient, but the victim does not want to disclose that she is being abused, they can still provide resources and referrals for the victim (when she is ready to seek help). It is important for medical practitioners to understand that abuse may not be determined or even addressed as a point of concern when the victim is in the examination room along with the abuser. Nonetheless, when it is determined by the medical practitioner that abuse is occurring, the way in which the medical practitioner and the staff verbally and non-verbally communicate to the victim (about her physical and/or psychological injuries) can determine whether or not she will disclose and seek out help. It is important and recommended for medical practitioners to communicate with the victim by asking open-ended, but specific questions. These questions should not proceed like an interrogation, rather as a point of concern and empathy to determine if the victim is going to open up about the abuse. Victims reported that they do not feel comfortable when they are being "talked at" or lectured. It is critical for medical staff and personnel to communicate directly to the victim versus talking "at" them. The victims perceived that this change in tone makes a world of difference for them, especially with their comfort level in speaking about or disclosing their injuries and potential medical/psychological aliments. An overall medical evaluation for practitioners (when they initially see the patient) should include a biopsychosocial evaluation reviewing the following: demographics, hospitalizations, medications, previous diagnoses, marital/family demographics, family medical history, history of substance abuse, religious and cultural affiliations, hobbies and supportive networks.

Based on the victims' responses to these initial questions and an examination of overall medical symptoms or injuries, a medical practitioner may possibly suspect domestic abuse and conduct a more specific assessment (previously listed) which can be implemented. As stated in Chapter 1 "Seeking Help", it is difficult for victims to open up and share, and their willingness to do so is highly dependent on the approachability, manner and disposition of the medical provider.

Research concerning from whom and where victims seek help is important for medical practitioners to take into account. For example, victims with a higher socioeconomic status are more likely to utilize a medical/private practice such as an office or medical practice setting. Meanwhile, victims of lower socioeconomic status are more inclined to seek help from emergency rooms or urgent care clinics. Medical practitioners should take time to get to know their patients' rationale for seeking medical attention. However, this task can be difficult for the practitioner due to the limited amount of time that the doctor is actually allotted to spend with the patient. Additionally, the requirements of insurance companies and the overwhelming amount (and importance) of documentation for the medical record leaves little to no time for the doctors to become more familiar with patients. The medical record is an important piece of documentation which medical doctors and staff strive in detailing accurate information with regards to treatment, prognoses and diagnoses. The medical record is considered a legal documentation in case of litigation, mediation or trial in a court setting. It is important and medically necessary to document accurately and review past records prior to a victim's visit, to seek previous medical complaints and treatment before an appointment.

## Recommendations for Medical Practitioners

- Medical practitioners need to be MORE vigilant with noting the frequent occurrences of symptoms or injuries indicative of domestic abuse as patients seek medical attention.
- Medical practitioners should NOT lecture or "talk down" to patients or pressure them to disclose when they might not be psychologically ready to disclose information of abuse.
- Medical practitioners have to address BOTH physical and psychological symptoms of the patient.
- Medical practitioners need to refer the patient to a psychiatrist or mental health provider when appropriate.
- Medical practitioners SHOULD refrain from providing a referral to family therapy.

- Medical staff and practitioners should initiate or assist in the development of a safety plan to keep the patient safe from potential harm.
- Medical practitioners must document all injuries or wounds that are indicative of being inflicted by another person, as well as the location and severity of the injury.
- Medical practitioners need to speak alone with their patients to protect confidentiality.
- Medical practitioners must exercise their obligation to be a mandatory reporter if the patient discloses abuse, in reporting abuse to law enforcement officials due to a crime being committed against the patient.
- Creating and implementing a comprehensive assessment tool for domestic abuse, if the medical practitioner suspects abuse of a patient.

These are some recommendations and suggestions that medical practitioners can incorporate in order to become more attentive and supportive when treating their patients who may present with symptoms or injuries consistent with domestic abuse. The victims that were interviewed by this author seldom utilized this formal support; as a result, there is less feedback and input for medical practitioners in this section. With that in mind, perhaps medical practitioners can collaborate with other professions and formal support systems to be a more proactive and sought-out resource for their female patients, who are seeking help due to a domestic abuse relationship.

## Clergy

This portion of the chapter includes clergy: priests, pastors, rabbis or religious leaders that victims reach out to for relationship advice or intervention as a formal support. There are some religious organizations or communities that have services available to their members that involve family/couples counseling or interventions. There is some controversy with regards to the different views that religious leaders take with interpreting Scripture, Torah or any religious passages that address domestic relationships. Biblical passages describe certain situations of actual or implied violence against women. Authors Colleen Shannon-Lewy and Valerie Dull (2005) commented on how the literature suggests that clerical theological beliefs may hinder the clergy's ability to counsel victims and the effectiveness of clerical ability to counsel varies greatly, as we can see from the differing experiences within this chapter. For example, there are selective passages from the Old Testament and New Testament that endorse male authority over women (Stacey & Shupe, 1983) and that causes controversial issues when uniting in marriage. Other religions, such as Islam, require women to cover their hair, wear modest clothing and women are required to pray behind men or in separate rooms. Modern

Orthodox Judaism can require women to be separate in the Synagogue. Therefore, treatment and restrictions of women in many religions can be viewed as a cross-cultural issue.

For the sake of example in the next section, this author will examine how abusers can distort and misinterpret Biblical Scripture. Theologians and scholarly researchers often debate about how the interpretation of sexual inequality and power difference are illustrated in Biblical (and other religious) Scriptures. For example, an interpretation of the male gender role depicted in the Old and New Testament can suggest that males are seen as superior, having domination over women, animals and all living things. This thought process creates controversy among theologians and feminist thinkers, as this interpretation reinforces a strong patriarchal system differing in gender equalities with males being depicted as "the highest level of citizen," thus creating power imbalances between husbands and their wives.

For example, in Ephesians 5:22–25 the following Scripture passage reads:

> 22 Wives, submit yourself unto your own husbands, as unto the Lord
> 23 For the husband is the head of the wife, even as Christ is the head of the church; and he is the savior of the body.
> 24 Therefore as the church is subject unto Christ, so (let) the wives (be) to their own husbands in everything.

These Scriptural passages suggest that wives must submit and be subservient to their husbands. If interpreted out of context, this can imply a power imbalance and inequality between husband and wife, reinforcing the likelihood of gender violence. This can lead both men and women to literally implement this specific interpretation of this particular passage within their relational dynamic. This does pose a major problem in partnerships, with men formulating potentially controlling and domineering relationship dynamics. Men, who literally *distort and misinterpret* this passage, do not see themselves as part of a team or marital unit. They often see themselves as the main component of the relationship. Oftentimes, this results in an unequal and unbalanced relationship, with the man justifying his beliefs or actions from misinterpreting what he believes Scripture is stating. In turn, abusers may choose the above passages and interpret them to permit and rationalize the abuse of women. However, it is widely known (amongst Biblical and theologian scholars) that Ephesians 5:15–33 was written with the intent to promote harmony and unity in marriage. Abusers who misinterpret this passage often segregate women from other people, resulting in them having power and control over the victim. This is an example of how the abuser *distorts his interpretation of a Scriptural passage to validate his abuse and mistreatment of his wife or female partner.* However, there are individuals that argue that this passage puts an emphasis on men protecting their wives to ensure their wives' security. Once again, it is important to note that Ephesians 5:15–33 was actually written to encourage harmony and unity in marriage. When viewed from a social perspective, there are many instances in the New Testament that attest to the equality of husband and wife with regards to their value in the sight of God. There are many other passages from Old and New Testament that highlight how both husbands and wives should treat each other, *exemplifying honor, respect and love for each other.* Kroeger and Nason-Clark's (2010) book, *No Place for Abuse*, illustrates the following passage as a type of guidance for husbands in the Scriptures:

> Husbands love your wives, just as Christ loved the church and gave himself up for her, in order to make her holy cleansing her with the washing of water by word, so as to present the church to himself in splendor, without spot or wrinkle of any kind-yes, so that she may be holy and without blemish. In the same way, husbands should love their wives as they do their own bodies.
>
> He who loves his wife … loves himself. For no one ever hates his own body, but he nourishes and tenderly cares for it, just as Christ does for the church, because we are members of his body. For this reason, as man will leave his father and mother and be joined to his wife, and the two will become one flesh. This is a great mystery and I am applying it to Christ and the church.
>
> Each of you, however, should love his wife as himself, and a wife should respect her husband.
>
> Ephesians 5:25–33

> Husbands, in the same way, show consideration for your wives in your life together, paying honor to the woman as the weaker sex, since they too heirs of the gracious gift of life-so that nothing may hinder your prayers.
>
> 1 Peter 3:7

> Husbands love your wives and never treat them harshly.
>
> Colossians 3:19

These passages suggest that husbands should have *just as much love and respect for their wives, as they have for themselves and God, as a result, to not mistreat or abuse their wives.* Many individuals take the Scriptures out of context to develop their own interpretation of the passages. As shown above, these passages can be translated and interpreted in differing ways as a guide to gender roles and treatment of each other within a relational dynamic. Oftentimes, abusers misinterpret and distort the context of the Scripture to take a male domineering stance, which they believe will justify their authority to abuse their partners. Many clergy and church leaders tend to lean more toward applying these passages when counseling the abuser and victim. Many victims do turn to their clergy for formal supports and based on the interviews conducted, felt that:

- The clergy tried to forewarn the victim.
- The passages that were expressed within the sermon were *motivating and uplifting* for the victim.
- That the church members/clergy were being *judgmental* of their given home life and were not equipped in assisting them in their abusive relationship.

## Forewarn the Victim

Ashley revealed that in her marital relationship, there were a lot of insults about her family, her career and herself as a person. Ashley viewed the church as being helpful and effective by forewarning her not to become involved in the relationship. Before a couple takes their marital vows, some religions require couples to attend and participate in a one-day marital course. During these courses, couples were asked to complete a personality test or survey to determine what areas that might be problematic and may need attention, or counseling before the marital ceremony in order to prepare the couple for married life.

Ashley discussed her experiences during this exercise with her fiancé:

> We actually had an argument on paper. We sat at the table with other couples. They had this lovey-dovey relationship. We are writing back to each other, literally insulting each other on paper. We were the only couples bickering which brought some things to light for the priest.

A clergy member (priest, pastor, rabbi, etc.) may learn about the current dynamic and the toxicity level of a couple, prior to his uniting them in marriage. At that point, clergy members can be proactive by forewarning the couple of possibly waiting or not proceeding with the marriage based on the results of the personality test or from witnessing contentious behaviors from the couple. From Ashley's perspective, she stated that she and her fiancé were in the midst of an argument while at the premarital course and doing the exercise that was instructed of them. Another clergy member also forewarned Maria that she and her fiancé needed to wait before they got married and they did not listen to the priest's recommendations.

Maria said, "The priest recommended us not marrying yet. The priest saw flaws just by merely talking to us." Regardless of the recommendations, Ashley and Maria married their abusers, even with the forewarnings from their priests. It is important and recommended for priests and clergy *to continue to forewarn couples when they sense "red flags" and to provide an explanation to the couple of their recommendation prior to marriage.*

In many cases, the couples will NOT listen and proceed, as seen in the previous scenarios. However, it is still important for clergy and priests not to discount informing and forewarning what might be damaging behavior for the couple's future. Even though the victims might not heed the advice that is given to them by their religious leaders, it is important for their clergy to provide their input to them. This is just another confirmation, recommended by a formal support, that the couples seriously need to examine their relationship. Many victims have their own vision of what they want their relationship to look like outside the scope of what any formal supports imply or recommend. This idea has to do with the victim's perception of how *she wants to change her abuser and transform him into an overall, better husband.* Moreover, this does not happen and leaves the victim in a vicious cycle, not really knowing how to escape it or get out of while in the midst of the abuse. The impact that a clergy member has on a couple can be very powerful. Despite the previous examples, it is important for clergy members to note that couples seeking premarital advice or counseling *do* listen to their feedback. Often, victims *do* implement the advice the clergy have regarding the victim and abuser's toxic dynamic, especially considering the weight and seriousness it has coming from their religious community. It is important for clergy to take note of the dynamic and possibly prevent future problems from occurring, thus the rationale for suggesting to wait and hold off the marriage. *It is recommended that clergy members talk to the couple, both individually and as a unit, to instruct them on their recommendation based on observations and results from the survey or test.*

Usually, the church will not recommend divorce, but may advise a separation if the victim is in an abusive relationship, which was effective for Natasha. Natasha explained that her church was extremely helpful to her as, "They advised me, when I told them about this guy, they advised me against it, and if I needed anything to call them." She talked about how other Christian or religious women, who are married and go through this, are scared to tell anyone about the abuse. As stated previously, the victims tried to convince themselves that they could fix the relational dynamic. Natasha shared her experiences when she went to her priest, who motivated her to come to counseling on her own, to discuss what he saw between her and her abuser in the overall relationship. Natasha said, "The priest was very helpful. He allowed me to come to counseling by myself and he talked to me about what he saw in him (abuser), what I did not see for myself." Naomi shared that her priest was motivating and encouraging when she came to him, "He encouraged me and prayed with me. I was crying and everything like that."

Clergy and religious communities can be a powerful formal support that can help, listen to and pray with the victim, who might not see the abusive dynamic. However, when they are made aware of potential or occurring abuse, it is important for clergy to speak up and assist victims. Clergy and religious leaders can have a positive influence on a victim, who may need the support from a religious and/or spiritual standpoint.

## Motivating and Uplifting

Many victims expressed that they did not share their experiences with clergy members (or other members in their church). Nonetheless, the experience of just attending church/religious institution and listening to the sermons or teachings were uplifting, encouraging and motivating for victims. Some victims simply wanted to listen, not share their story to anyone but take in the messages that were being delivered. For those victims, listening to these restorative and inspirational messages instilled hope and gave them the fortitude to move forward. Hearing inspirational messages and encouragement is what the victims expressed they needed at the time. Listening to the sermons or teachings, at their churches or religious institutions, was deemed extremely helpful for many victims.

## Judged by the Church

Conversely, some victims felt that they were being judged by their church because they dated outside of their religions. Carol stated she had been in a relationship with her partner for about nine months before ending it. She stated that she saw the image of her father reflected in her abuser. She expressed that she never had a nurturing relationship with her father, and therefore, not having a caring relationship with her partner. She indicated that she saw many key character traits in her partner that were similar to father, such as being a strong person and provider. Carol mentioned that when she reached out to her church, they were not helpful or effective with providing support, "They (my church) told me that I should not date outside of my religion, which I should not have done at the time, according to them. It was not helpful."

Carol said that she was in an angry state, and that no one knew how to relate to her. She expressed that she felt extremely judged by her church and that there was no real plan of active help for her there,

> Church members can only give you comforting words but nothing is going to actually, help you. The pastor seemed very nonchalant; everyone enforces education and I am all for it, but if you stand for something and are shady behind it, what perceptions are you going to get from people? My church was not helpful.

Carol needed more intervention, as she needed a plan to escape and church members/her church were not equipped to help her. She said that she felt that the church members and clergy knew what was happening to her, but never helped her through the abuse that she was experiencing at the time. Carol implied that she did not really trust the clergy, because their actions and words were not in alignment. She believed the clergy knew what was happening to her, however she felt *judged* by her place of worship.

Church can be an environment to provide reprieve and revitalization in a victim's life. Some victims found it helpful, prior to marrying their abusers, when the church was providing feedback of holding off or taking some time to work on the relationship prior to uniting in marriage. Other victims felt inspired by the messages of faith and hope in the sermons and teachings. In many instances, however, victims felt that the church did not know how to effectively assist them and they felt judged when dating outside of the religion by congregants and/or the clergy.

Earlier in this chapter, it was established that victims did not utilize medical formal supports as often as other formal supports. Similarly, within the interviews, there were fewer victims who turned to their clergy as a formal support. As a result, there were limited statements or feedback from the victims' experiences with medical and religious communities as formal supports.

## Recommendations for Clergy

- Providing literature as resources, as well as a synopsis of domestic abuse in the church's weekly bulletin and where to seek help for women enduring domestic abuse.
- Preaching about healthy relationships and teaching complete and comprehensive interpretation about Biblical values and the importance of creating a healthy, relational dynamic.
- Praying with victims for strength, protection and creating an avenue of awareness about such destructive behaviors and dynamic.
- Clergy and religious leaders should be proactive by explaining to the couple the observations of damaging and destructive dynamics within their union prior to marriage, and suggesting holding off or seeking assistance to make the dynamic healthier prior to the marital union.
- Devoting a weekly offering for victims/survivors of domestic abuse and providing possible financial funding for victims in financial need or support.
- Having guest speakers/educators teaching about the cycle of violence and providing ongoing suggestions that religious communities can utilize when addressing issues of abuse in relationships.
- Religious communities collaborating with other formal supports (that specialize in working with victims of domestic abuse) for increased outreach and potentially reaching more victims in their places of worship.
- Possibly collaborating with other churches (same denomination or interdenominational) to establish domestic abuse ministries in the community.

# 5 Judicial System

## Historical Overview and Where Are We Today?

The 20th-century feminist movement in the US protested a husband's marital prerogatives (Siegel, 1996). This movement helped bring about the repudiation of what was going on behind closed doors in family households. Feminists and women's organizations drew much attention to "crimes against women" and surprisingly, often found themselves allied with male law enforcement officials, who were also desirous of stamping out violent crimes against women (Siegel, 1996).

During this movement, "wife beating" became a term synonymous with the mistreatment and belittling of women. This term also began as a women's rights issue and became important to the legal/judicial system in legal processes. The feminist movement challenged the idea that family was a private sphere and women were under the control of husbands, who had the right to rape their wives and to use violence as a form of "discipline". "Wife beating" was already a crime under the categories of rape, assault and murder. Yet, in the absence of social movements, these domestic violence crimes had been neglected, lightly prosecuted and marginally punished. These crimes were treated, by the law enforcement and the judicial system, as less serious *if* they took place in the family dynamic and behind closed doors of households. Using the notion of "personal problems as political", feminists struggled to extract this form of violence from its protected space in the family and open it to public scrutiny as a crime warranting the intervention of the state (Schneider, 1994). Feminists argue that physical and sexual violence against women *both in the family and outside of the family* equally contributed to women's subordination and any violence against women was essentially against the law.

In the US, violence against women movements focused on changes in public awareness and in the legal system. These changes pressed for more attention of the problem by law enforcement and the court system. There also was a movement for changes to better protect women and to develop more stringent laws and penalties for all forms of domestic abuse. Feminists also challenged law enforcement's inaction and unwillingness to mediate such conflicts, rather than pressing charges against the abuser.

From early on, feminists and activists began to critique American society and shift to an emphasis of egalitarian methods and community-based approaches and services for women. Feminists and activists also began the process of opening up women's shelters to provide a safe haven for victims of violence. Shelters focused on helping women develop independent lives away from their abusers.

By the early 1980s, feminist organizations accompanied victims to court and sought to provide them with legal aid. Victim advocacy, feminist organizations and domestic abuse shelters were being developed and facilitated recognition of violence against women as a part of a broader structure of society (Siegel, 1996). This included many of the formal supports that have been previously discussed in this book. Formal supports include a variety of organizations with different ideological orientations and complex patterns (Tierney, 1982) from social service agencies to churches. In the 1980s, the judicial system was beginning to become educated on domestic abuse and jurists began to justify the occurrence of domestic abuse as part of the perception of "privacy and love". The development of this newer establishment of common laws was formulated by feminists, women's rights groups and women's support groups, who all advocated against domestic abuse (particularly behind closed doors) and for abusers to be criminally prosecuted (Tierney, 1982).

Historically, domestic abuse laws were preceded by political activism, which brought about many changes that improved the welfare of women and minority groups. Civil rights lawmakers began to enforce state laws in new and progressive terms. This process revitalized a body of state laws and increased the capacity of states to deal with social inequalities, including women's rights. Since the mid-1990s, the gender violence movement in the US has started to incorporate human rights framework following developments elsewhere around the world. Still today, domestic abuse is still stigmatized that domestic abuse is a "problem of the poor" (as it has been in stereotyped in the past) rather than problematic for ALL women.

## What about Today?

How have women's rights developed legally in the 21st century? The previous movements brought many legal changes to the lives of many women in the United States. Gender balance of men and women began to change, as we continue to see more movements in equality in pay, better treatment by employers, ending the abusive culture of bullying and sexual harassment in schools and the workplace, and so on. Current movements have opened more public discussions about inequality and oppression, as previous "private matter" became public forum. As a result, arguably most young women in today's culture believe that they have more options than their mothers and their options are just equal to men's options.

The formal support of the judicial system is comprised of local judges, attorneys, state prosecutors' offices and clerks of the courts. These are individuals that work for the judicial system in some capacity and have some type of interaction with victims.

There are some people/situations within the judicial system that victims identified as being effective and helpful and some that are ineffective. Victims perceived the judicial system in many different ways, as explained in the following sub-categories:

- Asking the Victim.
- Factual Evidence.
- Confusing/Lack of Knowledge.
- Navigating the System.

## Asking the Victim

According to the interviewed victims, it was most effective when judges *asked the victims* what they wanted to see happen in their cases. It was often surprising for the victim when a judge asked her what she wanted to see happen. In asking the victims what they wanted to happen next, this allowed them to reduce their fear of authority and to have a voice in determining the consequences, as well as developing mechanisms to protect themselves.

In Nancy's case she reported she had to get a restraining order:

> I felt the judge was helpful in my case. The judge strongly advised him (her abuser) not to speak because he was charged with a felony. The judge was able to pick up on his behavior and gave him eight months of restraining order right off the bat. The judge asked me *if* that was enough? I felt good about how the case turned out. I asked for a long-term restraining order. He (her abuser) has two years in which he cannot come near me, not even through a third party. If he were to ignore the restraining order, he would be penalized and put into prison and he knows that.

Nancy was able to have a voice and tell the judge what would work for her in order for her to feel safe. In Nancy's case, she even asked the court if the abuser could be ordered to take mandatory anger management courses for six months and random alcohol and drug testing during his two-year probation in order for him to receive help and treatment (at the arraignment). Nancy stated, "I felt good because they were able to monitor his whereabouts with an ankle monitor." This helped Nancy to feel secure that the system knew his whereabouts and were able to monitor and track him per his probation.

Many victims felt that certain judges were able to hear what the victim needed and those judges put in place some accountability and monitoring for the abusers, which secured the victims safety and protection. According to the victims, many judges seemed to understand what victims' are potentially going through … and those judges took measures to make the victims feel more comfortable with *results-oriented*, case resolutions. Many of the judges detected the abusers' manipulation in the courtroom, just as a component of how the abusers were able conduct themselves in front of powerful authority figures, such as a judge.

## Factual Evidence

Some victims were able to bring empirical evidence of abuse and stalking, such as pictures, phone logs, text messages and other things to provide *visual* evidence of domestic abuse and victimization by the abuser. This is deemed helpful for the judge to see empirical evidence of what has been taking place and the correspondence between the abuser and the victim. Jennifer indicated that she felt heard by the judicial system. She felt that by her displaying her factual evidence to the judge was an *effective* method for the judge and system to see tangible facts.

Jennifer stated:

> I pulled out pictures of teeth busted and braces holding my teeth together. The judge did not like him by the time I was done. The judge actually told him (the abuser) that, "I don't believe you; I don't believe one word that is coming out of your mouth." The judge did not like that the abuser had a restraining order from his old boss a year prior in the same courtroom, and the judge did not even know that. I felt so much better after receiving this type of help and support. I literally felt protected. I was devastated that it had to come down to that, but I knew that it was the only way it was going to go down.

When Jennifer provided visual evidence for the judge, to see "pictures of teeth busted and braces holding them together", the judge could comprehend the severity of what the abuser physically did to her. This evidence also helped in making the judge aware of Jennifer's abuser and his prior restraining order from his boss in the previous year. All of this visual, tangible evidence was built up over time. Jennifer was able to access it and provide it to the judge at their court hearing, resulting in a portrayal of what life was like for her. This is what victims need to do while in court presenting evidence visibly to a judge.

Jennifer had a female judge and shared that her judge who listened to all her factual evidence, made her day in court successful:

> he brought all his crony friends to lie for him, and then I brought my pictures, and he was trying to say that the hole in the wall was because of moving furniture. All the victims that went to the courthouse for a restraining order received a temporary restraining order with some victims receiving permanent restraining orders.

Jennifer had pictures of the damaged wall and her injuries caused by her abuser and she received a permanent restraining order, in which her abuser can never come within so many feet of her. A noteworthy reminder, *a victim must always keep the restraining order on her person in case the abuser does come close to her*, so she can contact law enforcement and provide them with it.

Many victims agreed that the judicial system empathized and understood them, as Katie relayed:

> The judge was very much on my side in a way. He looked at the information and said to the abuser, "she is doing you a favor," I literally wanted to kiss him, he said that, "you need to back off and leave her alone."

Katie felt that the judge was siding with her because she had factual evidence and information, and the judge ordered the abuser to leave Katie alone.

## Confusing/Lack of Knowledge

Some victims shared that the process of getting through the judicial system was extremely confusing, especially when they were going from appointment to appointment and they did not how the system operated. Katie described her experiences going through the system and dealing with legal professionals as somewhat "scary". Katie thought developing a website (of all the necessary steps that the victim needs follow) could be eliminate confusion within the judicial system for the victim. Katie shared:

> the system is scary and no one seems to be on the same page. It seems that people are misled and I needed concrete guidance. There needs to be an internet site to say, look if you are filing for this, here are the steps. They don't tell you what to do, but here are the forms, you need to figure out what forms go where. Where do I file? How do I file? I never knew that I could file alone. The attorney asked me why would you take off work, just mail it in. Nobody told me that; things like that are helpful, and they don't tell you that. I had to pay for this.

Katie felt very misguided and confused when she tried to figure out what to do on her own, especially as she filed for divorce and appeals within the court system. Katie felt that people expected her to know the proper procedures, when it came to her appeals and filing. She thought it would be advantageous to have a resource document or website that gives victims a step-by-step process of what to do in domestic abuse cases.

Melissa reached out to a counselor for guidance when she obtained her restraining order, since she had never experienced filing for a restraining order.

Melissa stated: "I did not know what I was doing; I got the restraining order and spoke to the prosecutors to put the trial in motion." She told her therapist that:

> I did not feel like anyone explained things to me. She (the therapist) explained everything to me. I felt like I did not understand what was happening, or what was going on in my case within the legal system, because I have never been in this situation.

Jennifer felt confused and she was uncertain if she needed to speak to the prosecutor or another judicial staff member for guidance. She did not understand the legal system or steps she had to take, since she had no prior experience of domestic abuse court cases.

The victims' attorneys were prosecutors, district attorneys and/or state attorneys. They were either hired or appointed to assist victims in the legal court hearings. A number of victims who utilized attorneys experienced both positive and negative encounters and these victims shared feedback (to this author) in considering which factors were effective or ineffective.

Victims found it most helpful and effective when the attorney *outlined steps and options* in terms of their case and *explained the legal process to the victims*. Some victims had their attorneys guide them, develop a strategic plan for a legal case and assist them in building up a case for court. Cindy articulated this process:

> this is our plan of attack. I was comforted when I knew that if plan A does not work then plan B and C; I could fall back on. There was a way to do things that needed to be done. My attorney was giving it to me in layman's terms and asking me what I wanted to do.

Cindy felt comforted by her attorney in asking her what she wanted to do and devising a strategic plan based on her needs/wants. In addition, Cindy's attorney helped in outlining and explaining steps, as well as sharing his plan to navigate her through the legal system. Certain attorneys assessed the victims' comfort level during the legal process by utilizing their education by having an outline, a detailed explanation for the victim. For example, "If the abuser did x, then y would be the legal result". Katie felt very reassured by her district attorney. She indicated that the district attorney could sense the emotional difficulty in the legal process of domestic abuse cases.

Katie expressed that:

> the district attorney was so helpful as she explained everything from A to Z. She made it very clear for me and that made me feel extremely comfortable. She was never condescending. She expressed that it was overall highly confusing (the system) and she was validating, warm, kind and friendly. She (district attorney) said, "It must have been very scary what you went through and this guy is scary."

Katie also shared that her district attorney had understanding and compassion for her, and truly understood her situation. In addition, when Katie stated that when she accepted the plea, the district attorney was very concerned and considerate in assessing if Katie was comfortable with that decision. The attorney gave Katie the following options: if she wanted to stay out of the courtroom, if she wanted her attorney to sit with her or if Katie wanted to talk to the judge. Katie stated, "She was very considerate; she did not expect anything from me, and made me feel at ease with what was going on." Katie indicated that her attorney had previous experience working on domestic abuse cases and understood how to handle the psychological component of what a victim goes through in the legal process.

## Navigating the System

Quite a few victims explained how they believed that they had to "navigate the system" (talked, smiled and were patient) with the judicial staff members who were assisting them in the judicial system. They felt that they needed to be especially kind and patient towards the judiciary staff and this produced more headway than being intolerant, impatient and irritated. Many victims said that because of this approach with judicial staff, they felt like the staff were more likely to be helpful and useful without a negative attitude. Maria explained the way she talked to law enforcement was careful and planned in order to warn them that her abuser was not going to listen to authority. This allowed law enforcement to psychologically prepare for her abuser. Maria said:

> I told the police, "look, he likes to be in control," I was deliberately pushing their buttons. I was saying to them, "he is not going to listen to you," and they were like, "oh yeah, he is. I am going to tell him how it is." I said, "Okay." I also said to the officers, "he things you are a joke; he is in control. He is not going to do what you say." They (law enforcement) did not like that.

Maria attempted to prompt law enforcement, in order for them to become more dominant than her abuser. The law enforcement officers did not like the fact that her abuser was not going to listen to their directions and what he needed to accomplish. This initially irritated them and they became more assertive with the abuser because of the victim's prompting.

Cindy learned how to navigate the system, so that people who worked in the judicial system would help her. She indicated that she learned the "tricks of the trade" about how to talk, act, smile and be extremely nice to the judicial staff, since she knew that they could make things go smoother for her, in terms of achieving her goals. Cindy said "It was intimidating to start. I learned the system in which to smile, talk slow and continue to be really nice, then they (judicial staff) were nicer and more willing to help. When you demand service, they shut down." Cindy was able to get things done through the clerk of courts, whom informed her how to file and where to go, to save time and extra work – this was a result of Cindy simply being extremely nice and patient with judicial staff members.

In the courtroom, Maria had to deal with her abuser showing the judge naked pictures of her as evidence of him not being abusive toward her. She indicated that the key for her and the main advice that she would give other victims is not to get overly emotional or upset, which may seem easier said than done. However, Maria illustrated that this was a tactic used in order to navigate the system. She indicated that she had to keep her emotions and self-control in check, particularly when the abuser falsified information and showed the judge embarrassing pictures of her, as well as making up fictitious stories about her. Maria recalled:

> I had to keep my stuff together. I held it together. You cannot raise your voice, you cannot scream, you cannot even get emotional and upset. The first thing that these men will do is say that you are crazy; therefore, you cannot make yourself look crazy. I was playing tactics with him. Whatever those pictures were, I did not know what they were. I told myself that I was not going to get upset. The judge did not say anything, she did not like that he (abuser), showed her that.

Maria expressed that she knew that she could not get overly emotional in the courtroom. If she presented herself as an extremely emotional person, that is exactly what her abuser wanted to accomplish. She strategically had to navigate the system, in order to remain rational and logical, rather than emotional or heightened. Regardless of what her abuser said or presented to the judge, Maria *had to keep her emotions in check in the courtroom*. Many of the attorneys assisted the victims with other legal services such as bankruptcy and referrals to private detectives, which were extremely effective for the victims. One of the victims viewed her attorney as a "father figure" and "my pillar". Cindy described the role her attorney played in her life:

> I am living in my house because of him (attorney), with the help of this man (attorney). He has helped me with my current divorce, mortgage answers and now bankruptcy. I felt like my attorney wanted to help, almost like a father-figure.

Karen had a similar experience with her attorney, who understood domestic abuse. Karen said: "My attorney was with me when the restraining order was issued. She understood domestic abuse. She understood why and when things were happening. She was my pillar. She tried to settle me and make things easiest for me." Karen looked to her attorney for help in protecting herself with the restraining order as she knew that her attorney really understood the dynamic of what she was experiencing.

In addition, Cindy had similar experiences with her attorney and explained:

> My attorney was great; he believed in me. He believes in me and was going to try to do anything he could. He (attorney) told me, "I will tell you the truth, this is how it is here. This is the best we can do here, and I know what you want, but it is the best that I can do for you. You know that I will fight for you." Most lawyers are not like that.

Cindy reported that her attorney was effective because he believed in her and she knew that he tried to do everything and anything that he could to help her. He instructed her about her options, the best alternative, and told her that he would fight for her and her case. Cindy's attorney taking that stance gave her the confidence in knowing that she had an *advocate* in her corner, who would not give up on her.

Laura reported, "the state attorney was a victims' advocate (like a counselor to the victim at one point in her career), the attorney, while being a victims' advocate, was inspired to become a prosecutor." Laura felt that because her attorney was a victims' advocate, she was educated legally and emotionally on how to help Laura and to even anticipate her client's needs and feelings.

Conversely, a few victims experience that their attorneys were ineffective based on the fact that the actions of their attorneys revictimized them. Rachel reported that she was in an eight-year relationship,

> I was a risk taker and he was not. I was climbing the corporate ladder and he (abuser) could not deal with that. He wanted me to stay at the same level. He would call me names to bring me down.

The victim indicated that her abuser was jealous and very insecure, since he was not maintaining a job on his own. Her abuser had significant problems with female figures in authoritative positions. Rachel highlighted that there was a lot of contentious conflict in their dynamic and her abuser would blame her for her failures and not credit her for her successes. Rachel recalled:

> I started to move up and he had a problem with it, he was at the same place. Personally, I wanted out of the relationship for four years. He worked hard on talking me out of not leaving the relationship. I did try to work it out.

Rachel recalled her experiences of trying to escape and having to use the court system in which to prevent stalking. She indicated that her attorney was not vigilant in terms of the information she shared with the abuser. As a result, Rachel felt revictimized because the attorney put her personal safety in jeopardy:

> I had to go out of my way to preserve my privacy as much as possible, and despite all of my efforts, it seemed counterproductive in the legal system. I told the attorney that I had to move and please do not say the address out loud because he (the abuser) does not know where I live. Within five minutes, she (the attorney) was saying my address out loud. I did not understand the whole process. The same system that was intended and designed to protect me, I felt like I was thrown out there.

Rachel tried so hard to protect and preserve her privacy and that she did not expect her attorney to give out her address so her abuser could hear it (as her personal information to where she was residing was disclosed). The victim considered this revictimization, as her personal information was not held in confidence by the attorney and the attorney gave the abuser Rachel's address, which would increase the likelihood of stalking. Melissa had a similar experience where she indicated that the state attorney did not handle her case professionally and what the state attorney said to her made her feel like more of victim. Melissa deemed this extremely counterproductive and ineffective.

> The state attorney stated that she believes this man (the abuser) is a sociopath and that he creeps her (attorney) out. Her closing arguments were five minutes long and you could tell something was wrong with her (the attorney). The state attorney's office froze and told me that I could not talk about anything except for the child abuse. The state attorney's office did a really, really bad job in my case. She never cross-examined us; she never clarified things. She laid there like a dead duck. I just could not believe it … the district attorney was preparing us as if he (abuser) was going to get off. I am like, "wait, why is she talking to us like that?" the whole time, "why is she talking to us in this way?" The system revictimized me.

Melissa felt as though her district attorney was visibly afraid of the abuser and a result, did not do a good job defending her in a courtroom setting. She reported that she felt revictimized by the state attorney, whom appeared frightened of the abuser. This led to her attorney having a difficult time in defending Melissa and resulted in Melissa feeling revictimized by the system.

## Recommendations for Judicial System

(Adapted from American Judges Association. (n.d.). Domestic Violence & the Courtroom: Knowing the Issues. Understanding the Victim. http://aja.ncsc.dni.us/pdfs/domestic-violence-the-courtroom.pdf.)

- Judges must listen carefully to understand the victim. The judge's demeanor demonstrates to the victim that they are concerned about the victim's circumstances and underlying events (American Judges Association).
- Judges should consider aligning him/herself to the victim's overall health and safety given the tangible evidence presented from each side and the ability to easily identify the victim versus the abuser.
- Judges must identify the abuse. Denial, rationalization and minimization are all defense mechanisms used by the victim. The victim's safety NEEDS to be the priority in a court of law. Judges need to understand the difficulty that victims might face with confronting their abuser in the same room, as well as the overwhelming intensity of fear, intimidation and terrorism that might resurface.
- Trust needs to be established by judges. The appointed judges MUST be proactive so that victims feel comforted, safe and protected by the system. The appointed and/or hired attorney can represent the victim and thoroughly explain options.
- Judges need to take a stance to empower the victim by asking her what she wants to see happen and how the system can help her feel safe and protected. This is important for the judicial system to grasp and for judges to ask a victim, for it may be the first time that anyone has asked the victim what she wants to see happen in the future.
- A victim may intellectually understand the legal issues. However, the victim is on an "emotional rollercoaster." As a result, the victim's understanding might be compromised due to her overwhelming emotions and confusion with the legal system.
- Victims do not want to feel like they are the cause of problems in a courtroom, and might utilize submissiveness and passivity, as well as defense mechanisms for fear of retaliation due to the years and years of abuse that might have occurred.
- *The courtroom must be free from intimidation by any involved members of the legal proceedings.* It is recommended that judges can use their authority to their fullest to enforce every relevant law in the case. It is also recommended that judges create a courtroom environment that promotes zero tolerance of intimidation. In addition, judges should not allow messages of defiance by the abuser and should enforce the abuser to abide by the court's authority and power.

# Part 3

# Informal Supports

Part 3, illustrates informal supports which include: family and/or relatives, friends, coworkers and supervisors/bosses, who assist the victim in abolishing the abusive relationship. In this part, the reader will obtain formalized ideas and suggestions on being a positive support for loved ones, what to say (or not to say), what to do (and not do) that the victims deemed helpful or unhelpful from their assistance. In this context, informal supports are individuals that do not have a professional tie to the victim; instead they have a close personal relationship with the victim.

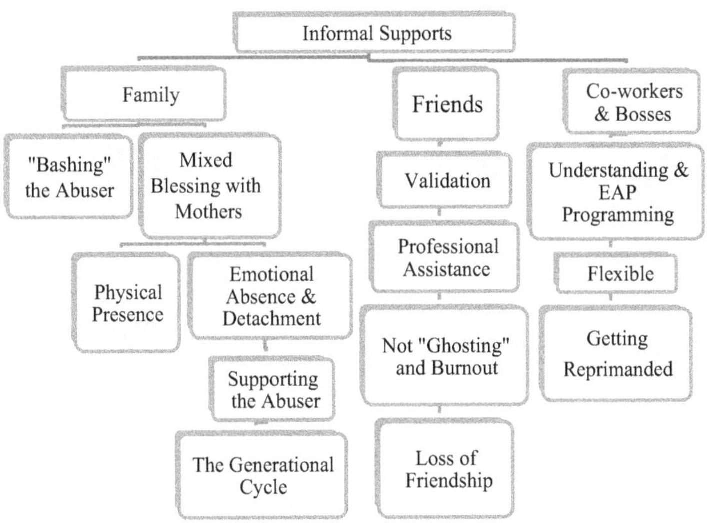


*Figure 6.1* Informal Supports

# 6 Family

Family pertains to any mother, father, stepparents, brothers or sisters or any other family members/extended relatives who are involved in the victim's life. Victims reported that many family members, who did not understand what they said or how they behaved, were deemed ineffective by victims. As a result, the advice or actions of those family members actually sent the victims right back into revictimization mode. Although family members or any other informal support members never intended to do this, their feedback and actions were contraindicative for the victims of domestic abuse. Historically, research has shown that informal supports, due to a lack of knowledge or being uninformed about how to support a victim of domestic abuse, do NOT know how to provide help or assistance for their loved ones. This section will help uncover how family members have or have not supported their loved ones through their tumultuous relationships and what steps and recommendations can be taken to be more effective for the victim.

## Bashing the Abuser

Some victims identified an increased difficulty in handling situations when their family members were directly involved in the victim/abuser relationship. In their interviews, victims expressed that when family members spoke in a condescending or derogatory manner about the abuser (to the victim), this created personal dissension for the victim with their family members. As a result, family members that spoke negatively or insulted the abuser were deemed unhelpful. The victims also felt the following: uncomfortable, helpless or hopeless about their situations and had increased levels of isolation and alienation from their loved ones. Again, the negativity expressed by family members turned out to be a lack of support from the victim's family. In theory, most individuals would assume that victims would feel comforted and validated by their family members "bashing" (i.e. name-calling) the abuser as a form of supporting and advocating for the victim. However, the victims stated that it was *not effective* when family members belittled or "bashed" the abuser in front of the victim for several reasons. First, families that participated in "bashing the abuser" gave the victim a solid reminder of the mistakes that she had made. Second, it is the victim's discovery that she might not have the capacity to attain a healthy relationship due to bad decisions on her part. This makes the victim feel unworthy and creates a feeling of disappointment she perceives from her family's view of her. Finally, "bashing of the abuser" was translated as a way for the victim to *increase her level of protectivenessof the abuser*, exacerbating the Stockholm Syndrome described in Part 1. As a result, victims often demonstrated defensiveness, rationalization and minimization of the abuse (to their family members) as a mechanism to have the abuser not appear in a negative light and created a level of *saving face* for the abuser.

Family members may perceive it natural or instinctive to respond harshly when their loved ones are being physically, emotionally or sexually abused by their partners. Family members often resort to vocalizing subjective, harsh feelings about the abuser to the victim. However, this method has been demonstrated not to be helpful for the victim, who is emotionally fragile and who may have conflicting feelings about the abuser. Additionally, the victim may see herself as "stuck," caught between her family members and the abuser. "Bashing the abuser" also creates an increased level of anxiety for the victim, who is attempting to manage her family's emotions along with the abuser's heightened defensiveness of her family. As a result, victims learned what to say and what not to say to their family members. They may be afraid to be completely transparent about their situations for fear of elevated reactions by their families (regarding the abuse and the level of pain the abusers have caused the victims).

Many family members refuse to become involved in any type of support for the victim because of the cyclical/repetitive nature of continued abuse and from the danger of the abuser's capability of threatening the lives of the victim's loved ones. Stacy indicated that her informal supports were not helpful, when her family informed her of what the abuser was doing or when they began to "trash talk" him. Stacy further elaborated that, "Informal supports were not helpful for me, particularly when they would trash talk him (the abuser) or inform me of all the negative things he was doing, they don't understand and would ask 'why doesn't she leave?'" Stacy began to quickly realize that her family members did not understand the complexity of this multilayered question.

When Natasha attempted to explain to her family about why it is so difficult for her to leave the abusive dynamic, her family members were also bewildered as to why Natasha would not leave him. Natasha gave a thorough explanation about why it is so challenging for victims to "just leave". Natasha shared:

> The abuser actually spends a lot of time grooming you, and forming a bond with you. The dynamic is so different. It is definitely not at all "cut and dry" and you begin to doubt yourself because you do not want to throw it all away, and blow it out of proportion. Other people do not understand this, all they see is that he hits me and that I need to leave, but there is a whole story prior to him hitting me that people do not understand.

Natasha explained that the abuser takes time formulating an unhealthy relationship, which is very difficult for the victim to break. Natasha continued to say that the victim invests time, money, emotions into the relationship, however, she believed family members could only see her being hit, so she should leave. Natasha stated that family members did not understand the psychological components that are strategically created by the abuser, making it more challenging for the victim to leave (as explained and elaborated in previous chapters).

Many families attempt to support their loved ones who suffer from domestic abuse, however, according to the victims, they are unsuccessful. When victims notify their family members about their abusive situations, the first thing that families need to do is *determine the victim's physical and emotional safety*. This will establish the familial attention that the victim needs and what can be done to facilitate healthy and ongoing physical and emotional support in their family dynamic. Families can truly listen and attempt to understand or empathize – therefore recognizing the complexity within their abusive relationships was deemed significantly effective by the victims. Families that offered *objective support, advice and suggestions* for their loved ones *without* "bashing the abuser" and not verbally insulting the abuser, were what victims deemed helpful, effective, validated and supportive in their lives.

## Mixed Blessings of Victims' Mothers

Many of the interviewed victims described a difficult and dysfunctional relationship with their mothers. This common denominator of a dysfunctional mother/daughter relationship between victims and their mothers is a factor that can be easily overlooked, but extremely important for both informal and formal supports to understand. Due to the strained or dysfunctional relationship between victims and their mothers, the victims experienced their own heightened levels of victimization during their childhood and/or adolescence. This is important to comprehend, as this indicates that many victims had already experienced emotional neglect or trauma *prior* to entering another abusive relationship with a spouse or partner. In this section, we will dissect how daughters perceived their mothers as "mixed blessings". The victims suggested that their mothers seemed *physically* present for them, but they had *an intense emotional absence and detachment from their daughters* in what they were experiencing. Victims often found their mothers were supporting the abusers, based on the mothers' experiences with their own husbands and/or partners. Finally, we will focus on how mothers who have had abusive relationships themselves set the stage for their daughters, by exposing abuse to their daughters, as part of a generational cycle of abuse.

## Physical Presence

Some victims viewed their mothers as extremely helpful in the act of being physically present for them. For example, helping victims move, taking care of the children, staying with them overnight, assisting financially and doing tangible or physical things for their daughters is what the victims perceived as their mothers doing best. This is helpful, to an extent, for the victims. However, the problem and ineffectiveness of the victims' mothers was demonstrated in an inability for their mothers to be *emotionally available and present* for their daughters. Victims who are able to attain the emotional support from their mothers deemed the emotional support and availability *much more helpful* than just physical support.

Monique indicated that her parents (especially her mother) were not emotionally present for her, but were there for her physical support and she described her mother as being like "Florence Nightingale" and stated, "My mother is great taking care of a sick child." Monique felt that her mother was able to assist her with the things that she tangibly needed and her mother was excellent at taking care of her physically, but she was clearly was unable to meet any of Monique's emotional needs. Melissa described how her mother physically drove her to the shelter and physically walked through the doors with her, however she did not show any level of emotion, comfort or compassion. Melissa shared that her mother went through the steps of orientation and physically signed her up for services at the shelter and she was there for Melissa physically but she stated her mother was literally "pushing me through the doorway of the shelter." Melissa could not describe any ways in which her mother was emotionally present and supportive of her. The fact that her mother was unable to meet Melissa's needs or acknowledge Melissa's trauma was disheartening and sad for her. The emotional support of the victim's mother is *essential* and *necessary* for the victim in terms of effectiveness and is much more desired than the mother's physical presence.

Examples of emotional support from a victim's mother may be defined as the following:

- Attaining emotional *validation* from the victim's mother.
- Expressing *compassion, empathy and concern* from mother to her daughter.

- A victim's mother sharing *and confirming* her daughter's feelings and emotions (as the victim sieves through the process).
- Showing *unconditional, positive regard and verbalizations.*
- Demonstrating *acts of love and affection* for their daughters.

## Emotional Absence and Detachment from Mothers

Karyl McBride, Ph.D. (2008) examined in her book, *"Will I Ever Be Good Enough?" Healing the Daughters of Narcissistic Mothers*, the importance of a daughter's emotional needs and how significant it is for those needs to be met by their mothers. She described:

> Daughters with unmet emotional needs keep going back to their mothers, hoping to gain their love and respect at a later date. Daughters who have a full emotional "tank" have the confidence to separate in a healthy fashion and move on into adult and have healthy relationships with their intimate partnerships.

Karen discussed the emotional absence and detachment from her mother:

> Emotionally, my mom has trouble being there. She needs to work on her own problems before she can help me. I wanted support … positive stuff; like with my mom, she would call and say, "You know, this, this and this." This is not what you want when you need support. You want your mother say, "Okay, yes, I understand."

Karen expressed that her mother had a difficult time supporting her emotionally, and her mother's problems often got in the way. Karen remembered that when she would talk to her mother, it was not positive in nature. Instead her mother commanded her on what to do. Karen did not get the validation and emotional support from her mother that she needed, as a result, she viewed her mother as being emotionally absent, verbally abusive and detached.

Natasha described her mother as controlling and domineering. The manner in which Natasha's mother and many victims' mothers handle their daughters' domestic abuse situation breeds a lot of animosity between daughter and mother and ultimately straining the relationship. Natasha's mother stripped Natasha's control and power, which was *not* effective for Natasha, and replicated what Natasha's abusive partner inflicted on her. This was deemed emotionally counterproductive and even *more* abusive for Natasha, which then affected her relationship with her partner. Natasha stated,

> My mother is a controlling person; very domineering. She immediately tried to take over the situation and tell me what to do. It bred a lot of animosity between her and I … mother was trying to come in

> and take control of the situation. It was very condescending because I felt that she was abusing me as well. She was taking my right and ability to make my own decision, similarly what my abuser did. She came in and tried to take over the whole situation that really put a wedge in our relationship.

Natasha expressed that she was attracted to controlling and domineering partners as a result of her upbringing by a mother who was also controlling and domineering. She said that in addition to her abusive relationship, she did not need a mother who was just as domineering and abrasive as her abuser. Natasha did not like how her mother tried to immediately take over her situation and her ability to think for herself. This was not helpful for her and further disconnected her from her mother. It also damaged and derailed any healthiness for Natasha in attracting an emotionally stable partner.

McBride (2008) described that "having a narcissistic mother, whether she is engulfing or ignoring, makes individualization (a separate sense of self) difficult for a daughter to accomplish." Some victims felt that the lack of emotional availability and involvement by their mothers made it nearly impossible to trust anyone and to fully individualize themselves from their mothers. As a result, victims looked to unhealthy partnerships to find that emotional attachment – a form of distorted connection – that they didn't receive from their mothers. Essentially, the damaged bond between the victims and their mother is *parallel* to the distorted bond between victims and abusers, as previously described in the Stockholm Syndrome section of Chapter 1. Furthermore, victims usually connected with a partner that was abusive or later became abusive, resulting from the detachment of a mother figure. Susan recalled that her mother was more into herself than her children. Her mother believed that her children were to be seen and not heard. She felt as though she was raised to be a victim, due to inability to trust people even in her own family.

Susan said,

> I don't feel like they loved me. They were self-involved in their own personal lives. Children are secondary … I was raised to be a victim, to look for people to trust outside the scope of my own family. I do not trust my own family, and then you end up meeting the wrong people, and then you are in trouble.

Susan struggled with the feeling of not being able to trust, connect or emotionally rely on her mother. She felt that she was more susceptible to meeting the wrong types of people and formulating unhealthy, dependent bonds with unsuitable partnerships.

Victims that do not have an emotional attachment to their mothers feel that they are more susceptible to having abusive, intimate partnerships. Some mothers do not understand the importance of an emotional attachment with their daughters. *An emotional attachment that mothers have with their daughters enhances the feelings of security, love and a sense of importance.* Mothers who cannot attain a healthy, emotional presence and have a detachment from their daughters compensate by only being physically present for their daughters. However, being physically present *alone* is not sufficient. It is necessary that mothers can sustain and maintain a healthy, emotional attachment to and sense of security for their daughters, in order for their daughters to potentially negate any type of abuse with an intimate partner. During the interviews, there were *distinct and strong correlations* with victims who suffered from abusive partnerships in relation to their own relationship with their detached and emotionally distant mothers. It appeared that victims sought out the attention, attachment and love from an abusive partner, of which they did not attain in their dynamic with their own mothers. *All interviewed victims described their having a strained or non-existent relationship with their emotionally absent mothers.* Victims described how their strained relationships with their mothers formulated a distorted and dysfunctional view as to what to look for and who they attracted in a partnership, as a result of this correlation.

## Supporting the Abuser

Some of the interviewed victims described that their own mothers were more supportive of their abuser, for example: making excuses for him, advocating for the abuser and "talking up" the abuser based on the mother's history of her own abusive relationships. Carol stated that she had been in a relationship with her partner for about nine months before being able to end it. Carol highlighted that her partner's abuse and control did not occur until four to five months into their relationship. She stated that she saw the image of her father (in her partner) and realized how her mother enabled such abusive behavior from Carol's father. She reported that she saw a lot of key characteristics and traits in her partner that she had also seen in her father. Carol reported that her mother was dysfunctional, based on the abusive dynamic that her mother had with her father. She said, "I did not get much guidance from her. She is like, 'oh he is just tired. He will be better tomorrow.'" Carol realized that these excuses her mother made for her daughter's abuser were the same excuses her mother made for her father. This was extremely ineffective, unsupportive and unproductive for Carol.

Carol stated that it made her feel that her mother was in support of the abuser because of her own personalized victimization. Her mother:

- Justified the abuser's damaging behavior to her daughter.
- Made excuses for the abuser in an attempt to keep her daughter and the abuser together and united.
- Normalized her abuser's behavior towards her daughter, by not being to eradicate her own abusive dynamic.

Carol emphasized that her mother actually did more harm than good based on what she observed of her mother's dynamic with her own father. Carol said,

> My mother DID NOT eradicate herself from my father at a young age. She denied the signs of abuse, instead she masked it by saying something like to me, "oh sweetheart, it is okay, he wouldn't do it again; it is fine." You are subject to think that this is normal behavior and this is exactly what happened to me.

Carol's mother told her, in words and actions, to accept it and deal with it:

> If my mother would have eradicated the relationship with my father years ago than I could have looked up at her much differently, as a role model because her actions would have been helpful for me not to subject myself to my own abusive dynamic.

Anita also explained the dynamic with her mother and how her mother would always "stand up" for Anita's abuser. Anita illustrated some of her childhood experiences with her mother and the lack of support which affected her in later adulthood with her own abusive relationship:

> I don't talk to my mother. She was in and out of my life a couple of times. She would always stand up for him (Anita's abuser). I have no relationship with my mother as she abandoned me when I was younger. She was not there for me. I called her from the hospital after he (abuser) punched me in my face and she was on his side. Now, I can see looking back on what my mother did while I was growing up. My mother exhausted the system, and her husband kept beating her up, and she would testify for him in court and they have been together for 20 years. She refuses to leave him and I refuse to have anything to do with her. I have not spoken to her since 2004, and I wouldn't either.

Anita demonstrated that her mother's relationship with her husband affected Anita's relationship with her abuser. Anita realized that she did not (and she still does not) get any support from her mother, especially since her mother was in the same situation. Additionally, Anita's mother stood up for Anita's abuser, and decided to stay within her own abusive relationship. Mothers of victims, who have not been able to break their own cycle of abuse, are directly demonstrating the same cycle to their daughters. Consequently, the victims (like their mothers) are conditioned to be in engaged in their own abusive dynamic. This is called the *generational cycle of abuse*. In the last section of this chapter, this author will demonstrate how impactful and damaging it is for young children to witness and be exposed as a young child (or young adult) to domestic abuse between a mother and father or intimate partner.

## Generational Cycle of Abuse

The generational cycle of abuse is domestic abuse that has been continuing over generations and generations in families. Abuse and victimization are learned behaviors, stemming from early childhood, pre-teens, teens and young adulthood. Research has shown that we tend to mimic patterns, even if dysfunctional in nature, that are familiar from the past. We also are inclined to repeat those patterns, when they are distorted and/or dysfunctional, because they are *familiar*. Families become accustomed to learning and behaving those patterns, even though they are completely unhealthy. This *cycle of abuse* is learned and embedded in victims during their upbringing and it is passed on for generations. Daughters and sons who witness their mothers being abused by their intimate partners will have a higher tendency to repeat those same abusive behaviors (and inherit the same victim mentality from previous generations). Witnessing domestic abuse in family environments is extremely damaging and scarring, no matter what age it is witnessed by family members. Daughters are more predisposed to follow the same pattern of victimization as their mothers who were abused. McBride (2008, p. 135) indicated: "it is important to note that you cannot completely 'cure' the scars of a childhood trauma. You work with them, process them, and learn how to deal with them differently so that you feel better." In order for victims of domestic abuse to stop the repetitive nature in which daughters become susceptible to their mothers' victimization, daughters must make a *conscious effort* to not repeat the distorted patterns learned from childhood. It is important for daughters to comprehend and utilize key elements in order to break the generational cycle of abuse and reduce the likelihood of being victimized:

- To note and recognize what they experienced was *distorted, unhealthy and dysfunctional* in nature.
- To dislike and object to those unhealthy patterns, to not repeat the dysfunctional, yet familiar behavior, and to learn to do the opposite of what was modeled.
- To seek out and receive psychotherapy early on, so as to *not* demonstrate the same patterns for their children and to learn a different set of patterns consistent with what is the embodiment of unconditional love.
- To conceptualize what a healthy intimate partnership SHOULD look like and how it should be portrayed, in order to achieve a healthy partnership and inspire a healthy, family system.

- To make an effort to have a bond with and emotional attachment to their daughters, in order for their daughters to have high self-esteem, healthy self-confidence and empowerment, and not subject themselves to or tolerate abusive *red flags* in their own relationships.

These are just a few measures that daughters who have witnessed their mothers being victims can do to break this generational vicious cycle of abuse for their own daughters. *It is imperative that mothers teach their daughters that they are worthy of authentic and unconditional love.* The best way that mothers can teach this, is by modeling it as a living example for their daughters so that daughters can learn from their mothers' healthy model. Mothers can verbally instruct their daughters of this paradigm shift and tell them what is healthy or unhealthy in a relationship. However, it is more powerful and impactful for mothers to physically demonstrate this by stopping or eradicating their own abusive relationships and embracing a healthy relationship. Mothers who provide this real-life example to their daughters send a significant message of the importance of breaking this generational cycle of abuse for future generations in the family system. It is a true teaching model that mothers need to provide for their daughters, in order for them to have a strong sense of security and recognize healthy traits to look for in a partnership. Mothers and daughters breaking and discontinuing the generational cycle of their own abuse are essential for the health of future family generations. Mothers teaching their daughters to love themselves, and to have self-respect in order to have respect and love in a partnership is paramount. Mothers do this by formulating a secure attachment to their daughters, that daughters can use when looking for healthy, intimate partner relationships.

Chapter 6 explored the following:

- What families can/cannot do to assist their loved ones from continued victimization.
- Having the family "bashing the abuser" was deemed not effective or unhelpful for victims of abusive partners.
- This "bashing" occurs so often in family structures, which further damages and destroys the victim's perceptions of self and family.
- It was illustrated how significant the mother/daughter relationship is in correlation with the daughter unconsciously seeking out an abusive partnership.
- The (victim's) mother's physical presence, along with an emotional absence and detachment from their daughter, was deemed unhelpful as the daughter examines her intimate partnership.
- Mothers who supported the abuser and made excuses for the abuser, particularly in their own relationships, contributed to the generational cycle of abuse.

- How the generational cycle of abuse occurs, due to familiarity of dysfunction and distortion in the daughter's family.
- Finally, the need for mothers to *show* their daughters the example of how to terminate an abusive relationship (within the mother's own abusive dynamic) and doing so early, therefore not exposing children to the abusive partnership dynamic.

In this final section of Chapter 6, generational cycle of abuse, there is very little research on how daughters emulate their mothers' victimization and learned behaviors of attracting partners that become unhealthy for them. Generationally, this can go on and on for many years in the family system. When a woman, within a given generation, recognizes the dysfunction and abhors it so much it creates a catalyst for change in not continuing the cycle of abuse for future generations. This paradigm shift requires awareness and *the ability to know how to change* this vicious, repetitive cycle that will continue unless women are given the tools and awareness to break the cycle.

# 7 Friends

Friends are often defined as people who are more than just acquaintances, but have a close rapport or connection with each other over a long period of time. These friends are people who the victims speak with on a regular basis. Victims feel close enough to share their intimate relationship details and receive life advice from their friends regarding the different spheres of their lives. This is especially true when victims feel secure enough to discuss their intimate partner relationships. Typically, friends offer support and comfort for the victim. In this section, we will examine how friends can be validating/empathetic in nature and provide recommendations for professional assistance. We will also discuss the tendency of friends to "ghost" the victim and how the victim's friends experience feelings of burnout, due to the victim's repetitive stories of the abuse. Finally, how all of these circumstances lead to the possible loss of the friendship.

## Validation

More often than not, friends and peers can be an effective source of support for the victim, as they are not as immersed in the victim's relationship (with her abuser) as closely as the victim's families. This space lends to the dynamic and increased ability to be more objective in nature, especially with the intent of assisting and guiding their friends, who are the victims in need. For many of the victims, friends who were deemed encouraging, validating and supportive (and who had empowering talks promoting strength and independence with the victims) were thought to be the most helpful according to the victims. In addition, victims that identified in having effective friendships *felt that they were being heard and listened to* during their most critical times of need.

Natasha shared that her friend would validate her feelings. Natasha's friend helped her in trying to make sense of her confusing and complex relationship with her abuser. She revealed that she and her friend would exchange stories, as they were both were hurt (on different levels) from their respective relationships. It was helpful for Natasha to have her friend's ability to relate to her and provide additional clarity for Natasha, regarding how Natasha's abuser was behaving and by the damaging things he would tell Natasha.

Monique shared that her friends told her that she was an amazing person, always validating her feelings and encouraging her to accept that she was indeed experiencing behaviors of an abusive partnership. Monique stated,

> They were explaining to me, that I had to stand up for myself and this was not going to change, no matter what I did … yeah, you need to understand that this has been escalating and this was going to eventually come to a head, as there was no way to avoid this.

Monique's friends could see her struggling in attempting to change her abuser's behavior. Her friends understood that the more Monique tried to change her abuser, the more hostile and volatile he became with her. Friends made it more visible to help the victim examine the signs of abusive behavioral patterns *by demonstrating and reframing* how the abuser was actually violent in nature. Monique explained that her friends were always encouraging her and instructing her to stand up for herself. They acknowledged that her abuser's behavior was not going to change for the better, but just escalate into more physical violence if she did not somehow make a change.

Many victims believed that they could not take their friends' advice of standing up for themselves with their abusers, in fear of physical violence and retaliation. Friends who offered validation of what the victim was going through, and possibly experienced their own domestic disputes, were exemplary in assisting the victim. In other words, friends who had been in the victim's shoes were *better able to validate and understand the complexity* in what the victim could accomplish within the scope of her abusive relationship. In this respect, friends offering validation to the victims and victims identifying their friends who were able to offer empathy and understanding (along with validation) were the most supportive. These friendships, according to the victims, helped them in attempting to separate themselves from their abusive relationships. There were also friends who did not experience that level of abuse (that the victim had experienced). However, as long as the victim's friends had a general understanding of the victim, and offered validation in listening to the victim, they were deemed helpful and important. Many of the victims felt that they were "going crazy" and needed their friends to validate that they were not irrational about their perplexing relationships with their abusive partners. It is recommended that friends provide *validation*, even when they don't agree with everything that the victim is saying or when the victim's perceptions seem to be distorted. It is important for friends to *support* the victims and shed light on things that the victims may have not considered before in the relationships with their abusers. It is important for friends to carefully show the victim that there might be other lenses to look through at the same situation. Additionally, the victim's friends can discuss how different perspectives may open the victim up to other options and opportunities (that were not previously considered). However, the victim needs to be *receptive* to these different perspectives and not psychologically "shoot down" her friends for these brainstorming options and suggestions. When friends attempted to help, but were able to realize that the victim needed professional assistance, this was well-received and deemed important and helpful by the victim.

## Professional Assistance

Some victims shared that their friends did not know what to do to help them out of their abusive dynamic. Despite their friends' suggestions, encouragement and validation, the victims could not move forward in escaping the realm of abuse. This is not uncommon for victims' friends to experience. Friends, who did not give up on the victim but understood that the victim's emotional level was too intense, too deep and tangled with the abuser, realized that their advice might be out of the scope of their abilities. This led to the suggestion of seeking professional assistance. As a result, friends who offered and recommended that the victims seek out counseling (and a higher level of professional help) were deemed valuable to the victim. Susan said, "My friends motivated me to seek additional support, without me even saying anything." Informal supports (such as friends) who suggested and referred victims to more experienced and knowledgeable formal supports were deemed extremely helpful and useful for the victim. Susan also said, "'You need help, go get help' … they said it directly like that and I thought about it, and said maybe I should get help." Susan stated that it took the guidance and suggestions from her friends to make her realize that she might need a higher level of care than what her friends could provide for her. For Susan, seeking out formal supports, such as counseling or professional interventions, was the next step in abolishing her abusive relationship.

## "Ghosting" the Victim/A Friend's Burnout

Friends of victims may not feel comfortable in being completely transparent with the victim and knowing how to go about eliminating the victim's abusive dynamic. As a result, friends not knowing how to help the victim any longer may "ghost" their friends that are victims. These friends will eventually burn out, because they are so accustomed to emotionally taking care of the victim, that they neglect themselves. "Ghosting" the victim can be loosely defined as when the victim's friends go "radio silent", stop responding to the victim, stop being there for them and essentially abandon the friendship. This is extremely detrimental to the victim, who might already feel isolated and alienated from her family and relatives. In addition, the victim might be receiving pressure from the abuser to discontinue the friendship (which he does not like), making the victim feel even more alienated, restricted and alone.

Prior to friends experiencing burnout and then eventually "ghosting" the victim, the friend needs to recognize that he or she may be experiencing burnout from the victim's repetitiveness and lack of follow-through in her abusive dynamic. Friends of victims, need to understand that they are (to some degree) emotionally taking care of the victim, which can be exhausting and draining for the friend who is providing the support. In some circumstances, where the friend is on/off "ghosting" the victim, the friend might find themselves out of the victim's life long enough to recover from burnout. Once this happens, the friend may feel able to resume their friendship with the victim. Eventually, if the friendship is not being reciprocated, the victim's friend tends to burnout again. As a result of "ghosting" the victim for longer periods of time, the friend may eventually discontinue the friendship. Again, this is psychologically detrimental to the victim. Instead of "ghosting", the friend to ought to set clear-cut boundaries (with no guilt attached) and set limits for the victim. In doing this and not abandoning the victim, the victim's friend can assist her to understand that she is unable to converse at certain times, but set some time in future to restart a dialogue (without the victim feeling that she is being "ghosted" or abandoned by her friend).

Recommendations for friends who are assisting victims, in order not to become burnt out or to "ghost" the victim are:

- Friends of victims need to be proactive in not neglecting their own self-care and their own emotional needs (particularly if the friendship is not equally reciprocated by the victim).
- The victim's friend should understand that she needs not to "ghost" the victim, rather set limitations on when to talk and how much time allotted to talk, and offer different suggestions in order to negate the victim's repetitive stories.
- Friends can suggest that the victim seeks formal supports, in order for the victim to get professional expertise to help them more efficiently.

If friends do not take care of their own personal needs and hone in on replenishing themselves (outside the scope of helping the victim), then the likelihood of them "ghosting" the victim is increased, resulting in a loss of friendship.

## Loss of Friendship

Monique reported that her friend became sick of seeing the same dynamic of her and her abuser's dysfunctional relationship. Monique's friend would say, "I don't want to witness this abuse anymore. You need to go get empowered, you are not, after all this time." Monique's friends (and other victims' friends) grew tired of and frustrated at witnessing the victim being abused and eventually abandoned the friendship.

Natasha continued to share details of her abusive relationship with her best friend, who tried to be helpful at first. Natasha would talk to her friend and express, "I cannot believe he did this to me." However, Natasha continued to return to the abuser and Natasha's friend would react by saying, "Why are you doing this? You are not going back there, are you?" Natasha's friend advised her not to return to the relationship with the abuser. Although, Natasha told her friend that she would not return to the relationship, Natasha eventually did. Natasha admitted that her best friend stood by her for the duration of her abusive relationship. However, the friendship was no longer close because of Natasha's back and forth behavior with her abuser. Natasha revealed that she resented the fact that her best friend was now married and had a child. Natasha indicated that she no longer speaks to her best friend, which resulted in additional hurt feelings.

Victims need to understand that it pains their friends to watch them go through these traumatic experiences, where the advice they give is not followed. Victims' friends no longer know what to do or how to help the victim; therefore the friends eventually disconnect from the victim and "ghost" her, resulting in a loss of friendship. Monique described how her close friendship ended due to her abusive relationship:

> I could not be friends with her. He (abuser) hated her. She would tell me not to marry him. She did not like the way he treated me. She would stand and represent us in our wedding even though she saw the abuse, she said, "I cannot stand to see him putting you down all the time, he would talk to you like crap."

Eventually, Monique was forced to end her friendship because the abuser did not like her friend and because her friend did not like what the abuser was doing to Monique. Unfortunately, it is not uncommon that the abuser feels threatened by the victim's friendships and forces the victim to give up significant friendships.

Chapter 7 summarizes and recommends the following for victim's friends:

- How important it is for friends to validate victims, in order to gain an understanding of/empathy with what the victim is experiencing with her abuser (which is deemed extremely effective).
- Friends offering suggestions for additional intervention by a professional (or other formal supports) can better assist and guide the victim to more efficient services, advice and help.

- It is vital for friends not to "ghost" or go in and out of their friendship with the victim, but should instead vocalize clear-cut boundaries in order to be able to take care of herself and not burn out. This may require the victim's friend to be proactive in finding things that are going to replenish him or her (and not resent the victim for mentally or emotionally exhausting him/her).
- A victim's friend should be honest and transparent about his/her NEEDS. This is important for the victim and also for the friend in not needing to feel the need to "ghost" the victim. The resulting loss of friendship can be devastating for the victim.
- It is disheartening for the friend to continuously observe the victim in a vicious, abusive cycle that the victim cannot break and that the friend cannot assist in helping her to abolish. This is both frustrating and exasperating for the friend.
- It is important for a victim's friend to note that the abuser might intentionally have the victim terminate the friendship. Ultimately, the abuser feels threatened by the possible influence that the friend may have over the victim.

# 8 Coworkers and Employers

Coworkers and employers are those individuals whom the victims either worked with/for at their places of employment. Some victims viewed their employers as a significant help with understanding the victim's personal situation. This was especially true after a victim disclosed her situation to her coworkers or employers and they then offered additional company support. Some victims indicated that their workplace environment was supportive and their coworkers or employers demonstrated understanding and flexibility in allowing victims to take time off from work to attend court hearings or appointments. Conversely, other victims discussed how their employers did the opposite and reprimanded them when they had to take time off, regardless of knowing the victims' personal circumstances. Undeniably, this added more pressure for the victim and this was deemed stressful and not helpful in addition to managing an abusive partner.

Some of domestic abuse victims who were interviewed were surprised regarding how understanding, considerate and helpful their coworkers and employers were when they disclosed the abuse that they were enduring. In this chapter, we will highlight the importance of how understanding and offering programming, such as company benefits of an (EAP) Employee Assistance Program (that offers free therapeutic sessions in a private, clinical setting) is a MUST for employers. This chapter also reveals how the employers' flexibility, regarding their time constraints, has helped victims in getting their "list of things" accomplished, in order to abolish their abusive relationships. Additionally, this chapter will also examine how some employers reprimanded the victim, which evoked more additional pressure and added strain to an *already stressed employee.* Lastly, recommendations are given for employers/coworkers to facilitate domestic abuse victims in navigating their future without their abusers.

## Understanding and Employee Assistance Programs (EAPs)

It is important for businesses and organizations to have their Human Resources (HR) departments assess employees' needs and challenges in their personal lives, which will have an impact on their professional performances. If victims reported that they were employed (during the time of their abusive relationships), they shared that their human resources departments *did not* have any knowledge of abuse taking place and therefore did not address this ongoing epidemic. Those HR departments did not create training or seminars about domestic abuse, however, these can be a gateway for the victim who is seeking additional, formalized support. There was also a common factor that HR departments did not address or educate their employees about domestic abuse. One victim felt *misguided* that her supervisor mandated a stress management program, in order for her to improve her performance and "get her back to being focused". That victim reported that experience was not helpful. The same victim also stated that her employer knew that she was involved in a domestic abuse situation, but her supervisor did not address any of the pressing issues that she was facing at home and her *dangerous living environment.* In addition, it is highly important for employers and their human resources departments to work side-by-side to better understand how imperative and impactful domestic abuse is for the victim/employee. Moreover, employers need to comprehend that domestic abuse in their employees' lives not only affects the employee, but also can carry over into the workplace. Strategies, security and a game plan need to be set in place in companies and organizations (of any size) in case the abuser shows up at the work site, which occurs more often than employers realize. An implementation of a safety and/or security plan, for employment safety purposes, can assist in keeping all employees safe. HR departments need to develop organizational policies and procedures, such as a step-by-step safety plan for their entire organization, if an unwanted perpetrator comes on the premises to harass or stalk the victim, additionally putting other employees and workers at risk of workplace violence.

Most businesses and organizations have an HR department that may offer an EAP (Employee Assistance Program) for their employees. This is a good incentive and benefit that a company or organization can provide for their staff. Most EAPs offer free counseling to their employees, paid out of the company budget. The Employee Assistance Program is an agreement between the workplace and an Employee Assistance insurance panel to offer a certain amount of free counseling through the company's EAP – with no payment from the victim/employee. The victim would initiate the EAP by visiting the HR department and getting instructed on how to access the EAP benefits of that company. The victim would also contact the company's EAP insurance panel, offered by her employer, to obtain a listing of psychotherapists, mental health counselors or social workers that are credentialed to work on their panel. The victim should be able to acquire the list from the EAP's credentialed mental health professionals and receive an authorization number and the amount of allotted free sessions through their EAP. After this protocol is followed, the victim can begin to research the mental health professionals' names, ratings and specialties. Once a victim finds a credentialed and qualified therapist, she would then call and schedule an in-person appointment. Some therapists or clinical professionals offer a free, 30-minute consultation with a new patient, to see if the patient would be a good fit and note the victim's level of comfort. This system is more comfortable for the victim – meeting with the mental health professional during a consultation to see if the therapist's style and techniques would be a good match for the victim. Some mental health professionals do not offer this free consultation, but it is highly recommended, especially when working with victims of domestic abuse.

Many companies offer this benefit from their HR departments. It is important for employers to communicate with an employee who is distressed and offer this suggestion, as a way to offer additional support and/or therapeutic services. It is advantageous for HR departments to begin the process of implementing a comprehensive evaluation and strategy of their employees' needs and challenges, especially when that their work is affected. This will prevent victims risking losing their jobs due to the stress in their personal lives. Oftentimes, victims do not seek out their HR departments for additional benefits and services, for fear of having their personal information infiltrated throughout the company. HR departments MUST keep their employees' information confidential, secure and not disclose information to the victim's supervisor or coworkers. In addition, as domestic abuse is becoming more commonplace (and its effect on the victim's professional work attendance and performance), HR departments should be proactive in offering domestic abuse training, seminars and resources for their employees who might be experiencing victimization. In today's workplaces, there are many HR departments that do not address and educate their employees on domestic abuse in the home and how that can interfere and transfer to the workplace. As a result, not only will this place the victim in jeopardy, but also will put other employees at risk, if the abuser shows up at the victim's work site.

## Flexibility

Employers who were flexible and did not micromanage or monopolize the victim's time were extremely helpful. This is especially true when the victim disclosed about her contentious relationship which she was attempting to end. This flexibility of time allowed the victim to get necessary court paperwork completed outside the scope of her work. Anita reported that her supervisors and coworkers made her life more manageable and less intense while she was at work. Anita stated that one day she walked into her supervisor's office and closed the door. Anita said, "'I want to let you know that my husband has not been a nice man. I need to go today and file a restraining order.' They said, 'Sure, go right ahead, I had no idea.'" Anita was upfront and honest with her supervisor because she needed to take time off work to get the restraining order against her husband. Anita's employers were empathetic and understanding and allowed her the flexibility to take the time off. Fortunately, in Anita's case, her supervisors were considerate of her needs and allowed her the flexibility to take as much time that she needed, in order to be safe within her personal life.

Carol's boss noted that there was a severe decline in her performance due to something personal that was interfering with her quality of work. Carol said that her boss pulled her aside a few times and said:

> "Are you okay? Did you need someone to talk too?" I was like, "Oh, I don't know what you are talking about." My boss asked me if something was going on in my personal life or not. She asked, "Do you need to take some time off?" I was, "Whoa, wait a minute." She asked if there had been a change going on in my life and what it was about? I could not think of anything, except, well he (her abuser) was having a great effect on me. My boss told me I really needed to check things out.

Carol's supervisor talked to her and assessed if she needed someone to speak with or even if she needed to take some time off. Her supervisor helped her comprehend that "the change" in her life was the realization that she was in a full-blown abusive relationship.

Cindy also revealed that her employer was 100% helpful. Her supervisor, being an attorney, helped her send a certified letter to her abuser, which was a turning point. Cindy also stated that having her coworkers know what was taking place in her life were extremely helpful. She appreciated her coworkers for not judging her and for trying to help her as much as they could, which she said took "a weight off" of her and alleviated pressure:

> My coworkers and my supervisor were extremely helpful to me to feel less humiliated and ashamed of my current situation. My coworkers told me how helpful my boss could be. They (coworkers) were in similar legal situations and told me that he was really helpful with them.

Cindy explained that her boss instructed and educated her in how to handle a stalking situation and how not to reinforce the stalking behavior. Essentially, Cindy's boss explained to her that the more attentive and the more times she would answer her abuser's calls, the more times it would give him ammunition to call. Her boss advised her to stop taking his calls, and to save all his texts and messages on her phone, without responding. This does not give the abuser anything to work with and does not encourage a dialogue or interaction between the victim and the abuser. Cindy's employer advised her to stop taking his calls in order for the abuser to eventually stop calling as he was not getting anywhere with the victim through continued communication.

This advice and flexibility, offered by the victim's employers, was helpful – particularly when the employers and coworkers knew of the victim's abusive relationship. The employers and coworkers wanted to help the victim to be safe and productive at work. Employers and coworkers were able to help the victim resolve issues that were interfering with work performance, addressing the situation with the victim and having the victim address the issue with them (if she was comfortable with that disclosure).

## Reprimanding

Some victims believed that they were reprimanded for taking too much time off, due to their domestic abusive relationship. This was detrimental, especially after their employers knew of the victim's dangerous home life situation. Karen, a teacher, stated that she explained to her principal why she was having so many days off school. She reported that her principal did not work with her at all, "I missed a lot of days of work, and that summer a new principal came in and she warned me about how many days I was taking off." Karen felt she was not supported by her principal, despite the fact that her principal knew what was happening in her personal life. The principal *still* reprimanded Karen. This principal could have with met with Karen and developed ways in which to *work with* her on objectives that she needed to accomplish and develop an agreement and understanding between employer and employee. Many victims found it difficult to disclose information and seek help (with regards to their abuse) as previously described in Part 1. Victims found it very difficult to disclose being victimized to their employer, especially when the victim sensed the employer was only concerned with the "bottom-line" (and not with their employees' safety and health). Victims found this to be extremely discouraging and disappointing.

It is recommended that the victims' workplace have some additional practices to keep their employees' health, safety and performance optimal:

- Utilizing HR departments to address the issues of domestic abuse, what it means to be a victim of domestic abuse and what to do in order to obtain necessary supports to end the abusive relationship.
- Employers can show awareness of how the abuse might be impeding the victim's work life (performance and attendance).
- HR development of policies and procedures for an organizational safety plan. This MUST include what to do in case the abuser visits the victim's work site and begins a verbal or physical attack and/or stalks the victim, which will also affect the other employees. This is

important not only to keep the victim safe, but also other employees who might attempt to interfere in the victim and abuser's interaction.

- Employers having one-on-one conversations (behind closed doors) with the victim to discuss change in work performance or attendance. Also, employers' ability to discuss possible personal life transformations and changes, and to offer additional support through the company's EAP in assisting victims in gaining additional formalized supports.
- Having employers that know the victim's abusive situation and allowing flexibility and understanding with her court hearings and appointments.
- Employers promote or assist the victim to begin the process of legally separating from her abuser, such as obtaining a court order to keep the victim and abuser distanced from each other.

Domestic abuse is worldwide – it knows no boundaries. Domestic abuse directly impacts the victim, as well as the individuals who comprise formal and informal supports and are attempting to assist them. This information from women who have endured and survived domestic abuse is intended to assist both formal and informal supports on how to help a victim in the most effective manner possible. Next, Chapter 9 illustrates the Empowerment Model and Theory. This is implemented in order for women to attain violent-free relationships and acquire healthiness in their intimate-partner dynamic.

# 9 Empowerment Model and Theory

Most domestic violence programs aspire to empower women who have been abused in their relationships. However, many community programs are limited in the types of programming, curriculum and funding that they offer, making it highly problematic for women to empower themselves. Julian Rappaport is an American psychologist who introduced the concept of empowerment into social work and social psychiatry in 1977 (Rappaport, 1977). He described that empowerment is designed to increase the degree of autonomy and self-determination in people and communities to enable them to represent interests in acting within their own authority. He further described empowerment as a process of becoming stronger and more confident, particularly in one's own life. Empowerment action is cultivated through professional support, who help individuals in overcoming their sense of powerlessness. In Solomon's (2008) "Empowerment: Social Work in Oppressed Communities" she describes how oppression and patriarchy are experienced by certain minority groups. This causes minorities to believe that they have less power than other groups. Solomon writes about personal empowerment and how it is developed:

> Empowerment refers to a process whereby a person who belongs to a stigmatized social category throughout their lives can be assisted to develop and increase skills in the exercise of interpersonal influence and the performance of valued social roles.

Since that time, empowerment has become a mission of service providers to help others reach their potential through self-actualization, self-determination and personal goal-attainment. Along with Solomon's definition of empowerment, numerous professionals have attempted to refine and clarify its definition. Additionally, researchers have made their own definitions and interpretations in community psychology. For example, Zimmerman (1995, 2000) and Maton (2008) describe that empowerment is a process by which people, organizations and communities gain mastery over their matters. Individuals, groups and organizations can all engage in empowerment processes.

Empowerment may be experienced as either a perceived sense of control or an actual increase in control over relevant resources (Zimmerman, 1995). Moreover, it may signify an understanding of and participation in activities needed to create social and political change (Zimmerman, 2000; Kasturirangan, 2008). Although empowerment has been defined as a process, no one has offered a clear articulation of what this process may look like. Kasturirangan (2008) offered a "Three Pillars of Empowerment" process described as:

1. Self-Determination.
2. Distributive Justice.
3. Democratic Participation.

Kasturirangan (2008) described *self-determination* as an overarching goal of the empowering process. Individuals should be able to establish goals and have the ability *to access resources in order to achieve their goals*. The ability to develop one's personal identity without fear of discrimination or retaliation should also be accessible to everyone. Furthermore, the empowerment process should lead to distributive justice. This entails a social condition in which both work and profit from work are equally distributed across communities and societies. In order to achieve these goals and support the empowerment processes, domestic abuse programs should be designed to address psychological symptoms that arise from abusive partnerships. Moreover, domestic abuse programs need a collaborative and democratic approach, which may encourage independent decision-making and enhancement of skills for all recipients (Kasturirangan, 2008).

Other researchers, such as Haigh (2008) described the word "empowering," in which people's lives begin to change as they gain more control over their environment to achieve interpersonal transformation. This also includes expanding capabilities and developing and/or re-establishing character strengths to achieve ultimate fulfillment and satisfaction in one's life. Individuals who need to be empowered have previously felt deflated, subservient and compliant, as well as controlled by others (Haigh, 2008).

Many who engage in an empowerment process begin from a place of powerlessness characterized by internalized devaluation and limited access to resources (Kasturirangan, 2008). At this stage, individuals tend to accept their situations as "the way things are" and/or they may blame themselves for their circumstances (Diemer & Li, 2011). However, through sociocultural consciousness-raising (Neal & Neal, 2011), people may recognize the need for more than just a distribution of resources. In addition, the empowerment process may involve the development of critical *awareness*, which can contribute to an overall understanding of the sociopolitical forces and access to additional resources (Zimmerman, 2000; Kasturirangan, 2008; Diemer & Li, 2011).

When empowerment occurs, individuals are encouraged to gain authority over their lives by increasing their skills, status and self-image.

As a result, individuals in the empowerment process receive and achieve greater rewards (Haigh, 2008). Although transformation is a lengthy and time-consuming process, the effects (with the help of the formal and informal supports) can be inspirational and long-lasting. This path of development and growth is visible, particularly to women who have achieved and attained their goals of self-empowerment. When applying this same theory to victims and survivors of domestic abuse, empowerment highlights a change in self-perception and the desire to gain more control over their environment, especially if there was a loss of control for periods of time. Learning new skills can provide the incentive to develop greater self-esteem and self-respect (for oneself and from others).

The goal of the empowerment theory is to regain lost power. Robbins et al. (2010) defined power as "the ability to access and control resources and people." Solomon (2008) describes power as "a process of human growth and development in which an individual, through his or her supports and education, achieves a sense of self-worth, identity, physical well-being and adequate and improved interpersonal/social skills". An empowered individual achieves the necessary attributes and the capabilities to be able to express one's self-worth, work with others in a collaborative fashion and to access mechanisms in order to establish effective decision-making (Robbins et al., 2010).

In order to attain or regain these positive attributes, an individual must be provided an environment that is conducive to growth and development. Ideally, an individual who is empowered will have a supportive network of people who encourage skill and technique building. This is a learned, conscious process – if an individual does not learn these attributes, power cannot be gained and maintained through one's life span. The empowerment process begins with consciousness-raising and self-awareness. When beginning the psychological process of empowerment, women must first develop a sense of critical consciousness (Lee, 2001; Freire & Freire, 2004; Kasturirangan, 2008).

The development of a critical consciousness has been described as involving a three-step psychological process (Kasturirangan, 2008):

1. Group Identification – identifying areas of common experiences and concern, a preference for one's own group culture and norms and the development of feelings of shared fate; having group membership and inclusion becomes a central aspect of one's self-concept (Gurin et al., 1980).
2. Group Consciousness – involves understanding the differential status and power of groups in society. For members of oppressed groups, this leads to feelings of relative deprivation, power discontent and a tendency to blame the system for problems relating to group membership. This understanding can draw connections between personal problems and social structure (Gurin et al. 1980; Klein, 1984).

3. Self and Collective Efficacy – refers to belief that one is capable of effecting desired changes in one's life (Bandura, 1986; Pecukonis & Wencour, 1994). Research on critical consciousness, self and collective efficacy is described as perceiving one's self as a subject (rather than an object) of social processes and as capable of working to change the social order (Fay, 1987; Lee, 2001; Freire & Freire, 2004).

The empowerment theory suggests that these components often develop successively and can be mutually reinforcing. These components can develop independently or in conjunction with one another. Positive feedback and reinforcement from support systems allow the experience of consciousness to heighten for identity development and reshaping. In this way, critical consciousness is at once a process *and* a cognitive state.

There are three levels of empowerment:

1. Personal.
2. Interpersonal.
3. Social and Community.

All three levels are in continual, dynamic flux, simultaneously affecting the individual and supports within the process.

## Personal Empowerment

Personal empowerment is defined as having high levels of self-esteem, self-respect, self-worth and self-efficacy (Lee, 2001). Oppression can destroy these forces of strength and direction. The first step in recognizing personal power with an individual is identifying with power that one already has attained (Lee, 2001). Personal empowerment can originate within a person, as a result of close supports or from those in the person's wider social context. One indication that people are living from a position of personal empowerment is the refusal to accept or tolerate devaluation of themselves or others (Evans, 2010). Therefore, believing in and respecting oneself is not accepting demeaning or devaluing behaviors of any individual(s). Personal empowerment is also refusing the belief that one does not deserve better or should think higher of herself. Finally, an individual in personal empowerment will not be subjected to offensive, maladaptive behavior, since this SHOULD NOT be tolerated in one's life.

## Interpersonal Empowerment

Equally important is the interpersonal context of relationships with one another and the helping of such support within formal and informal supportive networks. Interpersonal empowerment can be viewed in a relational context, which manifests between two people in connection with each other.

Surrey (1987) defined relational process of empowerment as indicating that there is a constant dynamic and ever-changing transaction that defines both personal and interpersonal (relational) empowerment (also empowerment in a wider, social arena). Relationship-building enhances interpersonal power. Consequently, healthy relationships among and between individual people and within groups of people (such as family members and other supports) is *vital* for interpersonal empowerment. The challenge in attaining empowerment through formal supports is the *discrepancies regarding power* and the *lack of rapport between victims/survivors and service providers*. In addition, potential biases may interrupt efforts to build connections and may potentially demean victims rather than empower them.

## Social/Community Empowerment

A society needs to be built on strength, contribution and opportunity, which defines the third and final level of empowerment. Empowerment practice is not complete without the attention to the needs of the individual that result from inadequacies in their social context. Nor is it complete without accessing the resources available in the community to answer those needs. When service providers help individuals to access and provide effective services, empowering opportunities will continue to exist for that individual, even after that service provider relationship has ended. Lessons of social and community empowerment and oppression are first learned in one's familial dynamic. These are lessons that never leave us, but can be changed through a process. As service providers, assisting individuals in building their strengths and accessing resources in their social and community environments (multiple social systems) can create and enhance supports to meet each individual's needs. Community-based empowerment practices acknowledge how the environment shapes an individual. Community-based empowerment practices SHOULD address this through collaborative efforts and relationships, capacity building, including formal and informal supports and networks (Wise, 2005).

## Empowerment-Based Interventions with Victims of Domestic Abuse

An increasing number of social service and intervention strategies have been developed, over the past two decades, to support women who have suffered from domestic abuse (during and after separation from their abuser). Some of these (previously mentioned) formal supports or interventions, such as shelters, legal measures and advocacy programs provide women and children with immediate and long-term protection and material support (Zosky, 2011). Counseling programs NEED to be focused on psychologically healing victims from the damaging effects of abuse (Bell et al., 2009) while implementing the empowerment process.

With regards to domestic abuse in particular, social work and counseling practices often utilize the concept of the empowerment model as an important, guiding principle in healing. This approach focuses on two key factors: the victim and her oppression. The service provider strategizes on the needs and problems of the victim, who is unable to cope effectively with stressful situations and to avail herself of essential, environmental resources because of her sense of powerlessness, helplessness and hopelessness (Hepworth et al., 2010). Many victims feel hopeless in their ability to get their needs met and cope with stressful and intense situations. Victims also feel a sense of disgrace as the abuser leaves them lacking power and control over their own lives.

Oppression centers on communities, groups and individuals in which social change is necessary (Van Den Bergh & Cooper, 1995; Payne, 2007; Solomon, 2008). Victims can move beyond the experiences of being powerless, helpless and alienated. This is done by gaining a sense of more control, purpose and choice in victims' lives by fostering growth and independency to make their own decisions. This model provides a balance of their rights and needs and thus enables them to make more informed choices (Schecter, 1982; Van Den Bergh & Cooper, 1995; Stark & Flitcraft, 1998; Dutton, 2010). Trauma-based programs that assist victims with Post-Traumatic Stress Disorder (PTSD) and Battered Woman Syndrome (BWS) (Walker, 2016) must primarily (with the help of supports) decrease symptoms of trauma, in a therapeutic manner before and during the empowerment process.

The main focus of these empowerment theories in practice for women who suffered from domestic abuse is to understand and strengthen their processes and context, in order to gain mastery over decisions that affect their lives. Many researchers and social science practitioners need to emphasize empowerment practices that might pose a challenging dilemma when counseling abused women, who request help, but who also express their wish to remain with their abusive partners, which is not that uncommon. As stated in previous chapters, when service providers are presented with this dilemma, the victim's safety takes precedence over all considerations. The need to establish safety measures and prevent danger from escalating produces intense suffering and points to the acute need for intervention (Winstok, 2011). Winstok distinguishes between "typical violence" and more severe levels of abuse and violence. Many domestic violence advocates believe that using this dichotomy is dangerous, as what appears to be "typical violence" today, may be severe violence tomorrow, leading service providers to believe that all domestic abuse causes a woman to be at high risk for severe violence.

As discussed in previous chapters, tension may arise with treatment providers when the victim chooses to stay in the abusive relationship (while the provider is moving towards termination of the relationship). This countertransference interaction may arise for the service provider as a result of the victim wanting to stay in the abusive relationship. The service provider does not understand how the victim truly feels or does not recognize the victim's cognitive processes for their behaviors and actions. When service providers "push" their own agenda and personal belief systems onto the victim, the victim may feel even more of a sense of powerlessness. This puts the victim right back to being a victim, with the inability to choose for herself and having a lack of control and power over her wants and needs.

There are abused women that wish to maintain the "positive attributes" of their relationships, while trying to find a way to seize or minimize the abuse. Service providers and formal supports need to facilitate a woman's freedom of choice as a means of empowerment, which implies accepting and respecting a woman's choice to stay with her abuser as an alternative of her decision. However, if the victim decides to stay in the abusive dynamic, the intervention needs to focus on identifying how she can remain safe, acknowledging and safeguarding the cues for escalated states of contention (for safety to remain the focal point for the victim). If the victim decides to make a change outside the abusive dynamic (by engaging in effective supports and services), it may increase her ability to make independent, cognitive decisions about her life and her future without fear of repercussions or further trauma.

Programs or providers that treat abused women SHOULD BE designed to empower a victim, so that she can make real changes even in her oppressive environment. The significance of supports and services is not just to change individuals' lives, but to also alter societal norms as a whole. The goals and priorities of supports and services are to be tailored to the individual victim. This author feels that supports and services that work with victims may need to change the way they view their own role in the empowerment process. Treatment should allow empowered victims to set their OWN personalized goals. The goal for supports and service providers is to facilitate and create options and alternatives for victims, so they can exercise freewill from a position of empowerment (Dutton, 2010). Effectively, formal and informal supports and services can play a vital and important role in reshaping a woman's empowerment process. The process is to systemically, progressively and individually teach self-efficacy to victims of domestic abuse.

According to Bandura (1986), a self-efficacy expectation influences the likelihood that an individual will attempt a behavior and persist in attempting that behavior in the face of difficulty. Bandura (1986) explains that self-efficacy expectations develop through accomplishments, experiences, verbal persuasion and physiological states. For women living in abusive relationships, learning experiences (that can enhance self-efficacy) might be limiting, due to abusers keeping victims hostage in their own homes and cutting them off from their communities (Lobel, 1986; Chronister & McWhirter, 2003; Barnes, 2011). As a result, these researchers suggest that these opportunities for victims to excel and advance might be severely restricted and sabotaged by the abuser. This may prohibit the victim from pursuing any employment opportunities and educational goals they may dream of attaining. Constant criticism and blaming (that is inflicted on the victim) is a component of emotional/verbal abuse. This blaming and criticizing can be a powerful source of verbal persuasion (suggested by the abuser) implying that the victim is incompetent in all spheres of her life. The abuser may convince the victim that she cannot succeed in school, her career or any other interests because she is "stupid, crazy or incapable". Finally, the abused woman's state of mind is often affected and dangerously threatened by their abusers psychological and physical tactics.

Abused women often experience intense feelings of fear, anxiety and nervousness, as well as other psychological symptoms due to the verbalizations of the abuser. In addition, the victim can be subjected to repeated and sometimes permanently debilitating physical injuries during the course of an abusive relationship. These psychological/physical states result from abusive treatment and can easily decrease the victim's self-efficacy and self-esteem (so they do not pursue their dreams). As a result, this keeps the victim from finding a job, performing work tasks, accomplishing educational and training goals and/or prohibits her performing successfully in different settings. Many women in abusive dynamics start out having self-efficacy, however the abusive relationship eliminates it, sometimes slowly, sometimes quickly, depending on the context of the abuse.

A woman who has self-efficacy has the ability and the self-confidence to believe in herself and to work towards making her goals a priority and reality. A woman with self-efficacy is able to perform job tasks, strive and accomplish educational and employment goals without mental and/or physical threats from a violent abuser. She is able to live a life that allows her to make conscious decisions and feel empowered by the choices that she makes independent of her partner. A woman who is empowered and self-sufficient does not feel trapped, isolated or alienated from her support systems. Additionally, she is able to communicate her needs in a way so she feels heard, she has a voice and she is understood by the people around her. A woman who achieves self-efficacy has a more developed and established sense of self and she better understands her wants and needs. Finally, a woman who has self-efficacy has *control* and a sense of power needed to achieve her goals *so she can live her life to its fullest potential.* She is an empowered woman.

# Epilogue

In my field of research, I worked with incarcerated victims of domestic abuse. Unfortunately, I learned that the victims of domestic abuse were often incarcerated for defending themselves within their abusive relationships. The more I interviewed these victims who were incarcerated the more I discovered that they were not able to easily leave their abusive relationships due to the complexities and psychological restraints that tied them to their abusers. The motive behind this book is to teach formal and informal supports/services what is effective and ineffective for victims who are enduring or have endured domestic abuse.

## Recommendations from Domestic Abuse Survivors to Domestic Abuse Victims

Domestic abuse survivors are women who were once abused and victimized by their spouses or intimate partners. Survivors were able to terminate the abusive relationship and they survived the domestic abuse they had previously endured in their lives. The domestic abuse survivors who were interviewed had ended their abusive relationships for a year or longer. These survivors had some strong recommendations for victims who were still in the midst of their abusive relationships. These recommendations summarize what was suggested in previous chapters. However, survivors felt the need to reiterate what worked for them to assist victims who are currently experiencing abuse.

Some of the most emphasized recommendations by domestic abuse survivors include:

- Early intervention, such as attending counseling while in the abusive relationship, might give the victim the strength and foresight to want to leave earlier (prior to abuse being life-threatening). Many of the survivors attended counseling after the abusive relationship was over due to Post-Traumatic Stress Disorder (PTSD) or Battered Woman Syndrome (BWS), Depression or other psychological symptoms related to the abuse. Many survivors explained they had to take their own initiative, to educate themselves (with self-help books or the internet) about their home lives, prior to going to counseling.

- That victims educate themselves on the dynamic of their relationships. As previously stated, examples include reading self-help books, online research, visiting chat rooms or online support groups and reading or participating in related blogs. Survivors felt that they needed to research: domestic abuse dynamics, unhealthy relationships and character traits of an abuser, in order to prepare them for the next step of using formal supports. Survivors reported researching online so they could gain an understanding of what was happening to them. Many of the survivors felt connected by researching independently, because they believed that they were not alone and they had other victims who were able to relate and define their experience of abuse.
- That victims communicate with their informal supports, who may also be a formal support by profession (such as a friend or family member who is a nurse, counselor, etc.), or as previously stated an employer, who was an attorney and who assisted the victim (his employee) from a legal standpoint.
- Victims should save the following: phone messages and texts, emails, letters, medical records of abusive injuries, police reports and statements, restraining orders, pictures or any other type of tangible proof as visible evidence in a court of law, which she can use against her abuser.

These are just a few suggested recommendations that domestic abuse survivors emphasized to domestic abuse victims as *critical* while in the abusive dynamic as opposed to after the abusive relationship has ended. This book gives first-hand accounts from victims of domestic abuse about what supports aided them to end their relationships with their abusers.

I have been honored to interview survivors of domestic abuse. These survivors were brave to share and voice their abusive experiences in order for this book to come to fruition. I am highly grateful for those involved in this process of information development and experiential life transitions, to be part of this life-changing research. It is my hope that this book examines the importance of the *relationships* between the victims and their support systems and services, both formal and informal. This book discusses and highlights the importance of knowing how Stockholm Syndrome affects the victim of domestic abuse and how it complicates the victim's journey when they are trying to abolish the abusive relationship. It discusses what prevents victims of domestic abuse from seeking outside support and services, and provides a voice from victims of domestic abuse who candidly share which supports were effective and which were ineffective. For those who support victims of domestic abuse (formal or informal), this book outlines how to effectively serve this population. It is my overall hope that formal and informal supports and services implement these researched recommendations in providing effective methods of action toward victims of domestic abuse.

# References


American Judges Association. (n.d.). Domestic Violence & the Courtroom: Knowing the Issues. Understanding the Victim. http://aja.ncsc.dni.us/pdfs/domestic-violence-the-courtroom.pdf.

American Medical Association and Treatment Guidelines on Domestic Violence. (1992). *Archives of Family Medicine*, 1(41). doi: 10.1001/archfami.l.1.39.

Bandura, A. (1986). *Social Foundations of Thought and Action: A Social Cognitive Theory*. Englewood Cliffs, NJ: Prentice-Hall.

Barnes, S. (2011). Black Mega Churches: Social Gospel Usage & Community Empowerment. *Journal of African American Studies*, 15, 177–198.

Basile, K.C., Hertz, M.F. & Back, S.E. (2007) Atlanta (GA), Centers for Disease Control and Prevention, National Center for Injury Prevention and Control. Intimate Partner Violence and Sexual Violence Victimization Assessment Instruments for Use in Healthcare Settings: Version 1, 43.

Bell, M., Goodman, M.S. & Dutton, M.A. (2009). Variations in Help-Seeking, Battered Women's Relationship Course, Emotional Well-being and Experiences of Abuse over Time. *Psychology of Women*, 33(2), 149–162.

Brown, J.B., Lent, B., Schmidt, G. & Sas, G. (2000). Application of the Woman Abuse Screening Tool (WAST) and (WAST)-short in the Family Practice Setting. *Journal of Family Practice*, 49(10), 896–903.

*Burning Bed*. (1984). Directed by Robert Greenwald.

Chronister, K. & McWhirter, E.H. (2003). Applying Social Cognitive Career Theory to the Empowerment of Battered Women. *Journal of Counseling & Development*, 81(4), 418–425. doi: 10.1002/J.1556-6678.2003.td00268.x.

Demarest, R. (2009). The Relationship Between Stockholm Syndrome and Post-Traumatic Stress Disorder in Battered Women. *Inquiries Journal: Social Science, Arts & Humanities*, 1(11), 1/1.

Diemer, M.A. & Li, C.H. (2011). Critical Consciousness Development and Political Participation among Marginalized Youth. *Child Development*, 82(6), 1815–1833. doi: 10.1111/j.1467-8624.2011.01650.x.

Dutton, D. (2010). The Gender Paradigm and the Architecture of Antiscience. *Partner Abuse*, 1(1). www.Springerpub.connect.com. doi: 10.1891/1946-6560.1.1.5

Dutton, D.G. & Painter, S. (1993). Emotional Attachment in Abusive Relationships: A Test of Traumatic Bonding Theory. *Violence Victim*, 8, 105–120.

Evans, P. (2010). *The Verbally Abusive Relationship: How to Recognize It and How to Respond*. Holbrook, Mass: Adams.

Farrington, M. & Hacker, R. (1995). A Scale for Identifying "Stockholm Syndrome" Reactions in Young Dating Women: Factor Structure Reliability, and Validity. *Violence and Victims*, 10(1), 3–22.

Fay, B. (1987). *Critical Social Science: Liberation and Its Limits*. Ithaca, NY: Cornell University Press.

Feldhaus, K.M., Koziol-McLain, J., Amsbury, H.L., Norton, I.M., Lowenstein, S.R. & Abbot, J.T. (1997). Accuracy of 3 Brief Screening Questions for Detecting Partner Violence in the Emergency Department. *Journal of the American Medical Association*, 277, 1357–1361.

Freire, P. & Freire, A. (2004). *Pedagogy of Hope: Reliving Pedagogy of the Oppressed*. London & New York, NY: The Continuum Publishing Company.

Graham, D.L., Rawlings, E.I., Ihms, K., Latimer, D., Foliano, J., Thompson, A. & Sutton, K. (1995). A Scale for Identifying "Stockholm Syndrome" Reactions in Young Dating Women. *Factor Structure, Reliability, and Validity, Violence and Victims*, 10, 3–22.

Gurin, P., Miller, A. & Gurin, G. (1980). Stratum Identification and Consciousness. *Social Psychology Quarterly*, 43, 30–47. doi: 10.2307/3033746.

Haigh, C.A. (2008). Exploring the Evidence Baseof Patient Involvement in the Management of Health Care Services. *Journal of Nursing Management*, 16(4), 452–462. doi: 10.1111/j.1365-2834.2008.00865.x.

Hepworth, D.H., Rooney, R., Rooney, G., Larson, J. & Gottfried, K.S. (2010). *Direct Social Work Practice. Theory and Skills* (8th ed.). Pacific Grove, CA: Brooks/Cole.

Kasturirangan, A. (2008). Empowerment and Programs to Designed to Address Domestic Violence. *Violence Against Women*, 14(12), 1465–1475.

Kirkwood, C. (1993). *Leaving Abusive Partners: From the Scars of Survival to the Wisdom for Change*. London: Sage Publications.

Klein, E. (1984). Gender Politics from Consciousness to Mass Politics. https://philpapers.org/rec/KLEGPF-2.

Kroeger, C.C. & Nason-Clark, N. (2010). *No Place for Abuse: Biblical & Practical Resources to Counteract Domestic Violence*. Downers Grove, IL: IVP Books.

Lambert, L. (2019). *Encyclopedia Britannica*. Stockholm Syndrome. Psychology.

Lee, J. (2001). *The Empowerment Approach to Social Work Practice: Building the Beloved Community* (2nd ed.). New York, NY: Columbia University Press.

Lobel, K. (1986). *Naming the Violence: Speaking Out About Lesbian Battering*. New York, NY: Seal Press.

Maton, K.I. (2008). Empowering Community Settings: Agents of Individual Development, Community Betterment and Positive Social Change. *American Journal of Community Psychology*, 41, 4–21.

McBride, K. (2008). *"Will I Ever Be Good Enough?" Healing the Daughters of Narcissistic Mothers*. New York, NY: Atria Paperback.

Mills, L. (1998). Mandatory Arrest and Prosecution Policies for Domestic Violence: A Critical Literature Review and Case for More Research to Test Victim Empowerment Approaches. *Criminal Justice and Behavior*, 25(3), 306–318.

Neal, J.W. & Neal, Z.P. (2011). Power as a Structural Phenomenon. *American Journal of Community Psychology*, 48(3–4), 157–167. doi: 10.1007/s10464-010-9356.3.

New Testament of the Bible: Ephesians 5:22–25; Ephesians 5: 15–33; 1 Peter 3:7; Colossians 3:19.

Payne, M. (2007). *What is Professional Social Work?* (rev. 2nd ed.). Chicago, IL: Lyceum Books.

Pecukonis, E. & Wencour, S. (1994). Perceptions of Self & Collective Efficacy in Community Organization Theory & Practice. *Journal of Community Practice*, 1(2), 5–21.

Rabin, R.F., Jennings, J.M., Campbell, J.C. & Bair-Merritt, M.C. (2009). Intimate Partner Violence Screening Tools: A Systematic Review. *Journal of Preventive Medicine*, Elsevier, Inc. 36(5), 439–444.

Rappaport, J. (1977). *Community Psychology: Values, Research and Action*. San Diego, CA: Harcourt School.

Robbins, S.P., Chatterjee, P. & Canda, E.R. (2010). *Contemporary Human Behavior Therapy: A Critical Perspective on Social Work* (2nd ed.). Boston, MA: Pearson Education, Inc.

Schecter, S. (1982). *Women and Male Violence: The Visions and Struggles of the Battered Women's Movement*. Boston, MA: South End Press.

Schneider, C.E. (1994). Marriage, Morals and the Law: No-fault Divorce and Moral Discourse. *Utah Law Review*, 2, 503–585.

Shannon-Lewy, C. & Dull, V.T. (2005). The Response of Christian Clergy to Domestic Violence: Help or Hindrance? *Aggression and Violent Behavior*, 10(6), 647–659.

Siegel, R.B. (1996). "The Rule of Love:" Wife Beating as Prerogative and Privacy. *Yale Law Review*, 105(8), 2117. doi: 10.2307/797286.

*Sleeping with the Enemy*. (1991). Directed by Joseph Ruben.

Solomon, B. (2008). Empowerment: Social Work in Oppressed Communities. *Journal of Social Work Practice: Psychotherapeutic Approaches in Health, Welfare and the Community*, 79–91. doi: 10.1080/02650538708414984.

Stacey, W. & Shupe, A. (1983). *The Family Secret: Family Violence in America*. Boston, MA: Beacon Press.

Stark, E. & Flitcraft, A.H. (1998). Women Battering. In R.B. Wallace (Ed.), *Maxcy-Rosenau-Last Public Health and Preventive Medicine* (14th ed.). East Norwalk, CT: Appleton & Lange, 1231–1238.

Surrey, J. (1987). *Relationship and Empowerment*. Wellesley, MA: Stone Center for Developmental Services and Studies.

Tierney, K.J. (1982). The Battered Women Movement and Creation of the Wife Beating Problem. *Social Problems*, 29(3), 207–220.

Van Den Bergh, N. & Cooper, L.B. (1995). Introduction to Feminist Visions for Social Work. In J.E. Tropman, J.L. Erlich & J. Rothman (Eds.), *Tactics & Techniques of Community Intervention*. Itasca, IL: Peacock, 74–93.

Walker, L.E. (1991). Posttraumatic Stress Disorder in Women: Diagnosis and Treatment of Battered Woman Syndrome. *Psychotherapy, Theory, Research, Practice and Training*, 28, 21–29. doi: 10.1037/0033-3204.28.1.21. psychnet.apa.org.

Walker, L.E. (2016). *The Battered Woman Syndrome* (4th ed.). New York, NY: Springer.

Wallace, P. (2007). How Can She Still Love Him? Domestic Violence and the Stockholm Syndrome. *Community Practitioner*, 80(10), 32–34.

Wasson, J.H., Jette, A.M., Anderson, J., Johnson, D.J., Nelson, E.C. & Kilo, C.M. (2000). Routine, Single-Item Screening to Identify Abusive Relationships in Women. *The Journal of Family Practice*, 49, 1017–1022.

Winstok, Z. (2011). The Effects of Sex and Severity of Aggression on Formal and Informal Social Agents' Involvement in Partner Abuse. *American Journal of Men's Health*, 6(2), 136–145.

Wise, J.B. (2005). *Empowerment Practice with Families in Distress*. New York, NY: Columbia University Press.

Zimmerman, M.A. (1995). Psychological Empowerment Issues and Illustrations. *American Journal of Community Psychology*, 23(5), 581–599. doi: 10.1007/BF02506983.
Zimmerman, M.A. (2000). Empowerment Theory: Psychological, Organizational and Community Levels of Analysis. In J. Rappaport & E. Seidman (Eds.), *Handbook of Community Psychology*. New York, NY: Springer Science & Business Media.
Zosky, D. (2011). A Matter of Life or Death: The Voices of Domestic Violence Survivors. *Affilia-Journal of Women and Social Work*, 26(2), 201–212. doi: 10.1177/0886109911405494.

# Index

For Product Safety Concerns and Information please contact our EU representative GPSR@taylorandfrancis.com
Taylor & Francis Verlag GmbH, Kaufingerstraße 24, 80331 München, Germany

www.ingramcontent.com/pod-product-compliance
Ingram Content Group UK Ltd.
Pitfield, Milton Keynes, MK11 3LW, UK
UKHW021958180926
475701UK00003B/76
*9780367859589*